10637340

Country Music Comin' Home

James C. Hefley

Jefferson Twp Library
1031 Weldon Road
Oak Ridge, N.J. 07438
973-208-6244
www.jeffersonlibrary.net

Copyright James C. Hefley, 1995, 2009
All Rights Reserved.

Printed in the United States of America
by Lightning Source
Cover design by Cyndi Allison
Library of Congress Control Number: 92-074767
ISBN 0-929292-27-8
Scripture references are from the King James Version
of the Bible.

Hannibal Books
P.O. Box 461592
Garland, Texas 75046
1-800-747-0738
www.hannibalbooks.com

(To order more copies of *Country Music Comin' Home* mail a
check for $12.95 plus $4 shipping, with 50 cents extra for each
additional book—to Hannibal Books at the address above.)

Dedication

*This book is dedicated
to the memory of my daddy, Fred Hefley,
and to his singing buddy, Greg Cantrell,
who still loves the old songs.*

Contents

Chapter 1
Country Music in Big Creek Valley

Some 50 years have passed, although the event seems as though it was yesterday. We'd known all week we would be going to the Kents' late Saturday afternoon to listen to the Grand Ole Opry. Milton and Nola Kent had a battery radio— the first in upper Big Creek Valley in Newton County, AR. The Kents lived only a half-mile down the creek, so we'd walk.

Daddy slopped the hogs, milked and fed the cows, and took care of the horses. Mama wrapped up the twin babies, Louise and Loucille, while my impish little brother, Howard, and I squirmed impatiently on the porch of our log cabin. Daddy's guitar lay between us. It was packed in its black case. Under no condition were we to open the case. I was all of 6-years old. Howard was 3.

For the hundredth time I asked Mama, "When air we leavin' fer Milton and Nola's?"

Mama gave the same answer; "When your daddy gets done at the barn."

Finally we heard Daddy walking in from the barn and singing, "Way back in the hills . . . where as a boy I wandered . . .." He was singing loud enough to be heard a mile down the creek.

"Got the younguns ready, Hester?" he hollered.

Mama emerged from the cabin and carried a baby under

each arm. Daddy grabbed up the guitar and took one of the twins. We started down the path. I proudly led the way as I swung the lantern. Brother trooped along between Mama and Daddy. Daddy smiled up at the blue sky. "Hain't gonna be no static tonight. Hit'l be lack we're right thar on the Opry stage."

We stopped en route and picked up Grampa Tom Hefley. Grampa lived in the log house his grandfather, Tom Tennison, had built in 1858. My grandpa had been powerful lonesome in the two years since Grandma Eller died.

Grampa picked up his fiddle. "Maybe I'll hit a lick or two with them Opry fellers," he said.

We took the trail that rimmed the wooded side of Grampa's cornfield. Halfway to the Kents' we caught up with Uncle Elmer, Aunt Viola, and their two boys, Athel and E.L. Athel clutched his fiddle under one arm.

The house already was half full by the time we edged through the door. Brother and I plopped down on the floor before the big Philco walnut console as we anticipated the sweet music we were about to hear. Uncle Willie Pink, my favorite storyteller, was in the middle of a panther yarn when a reverent hush began settling over the room. The magic moment was near.

Milton Kent frowned at Uncle Willie, who was still rattling. "Kin ya hold the rest of that story a while, Pink? Hit's 'most time for the Opry."

Milton checked his watch and clicked on the radio. He'd kept it off to save the batteries. The mellow-toned announcer sounded as if he were right in front of us: "This is your clear-channel station, WSM, from Nashville, Tennessee. The time at the tone will be eight p.m."

I took a deep breath and then heard: "Ladies and gentlemen, welcome to the Grand Ole Opry. Here is your host, the Solemn Ole Judge George D. Hay."

Opry Sing Along

Oh, what wonders of sound we heard that night! Uncle Dave Macon led a hoedown with his fiddle. Young Bill Monroe and his Bluegrass Boys from Kentucky harmonized about funny Uncle Pen. Then we heard the Crook Brothers, the Fruit Jar Drinkers, the Clodhoppers, Zeke Clements and the Bronco Busters, and Roy Acuff making foot-stompin' music from more than 400 miles away.

Grampa Tom and Cousin Athel accompanied Uncle Dave on their fiddles. Daddy played his guitar and sang with Roy Acuff:

What a beautiful thought I am thinking
Concerning a great speckled bird.
Remember her name is recorded
On the pages of God's holy Word.

"That's right out of the Bible," Roy said. "Comes from the ninth verse in the 12th chapter of the Book of Jeremiah."

By 10 o'clock babies were sleeping on every bed in the house. Mama wanted to gather up the twins and take them home. "Please, Mama, let's stay and hear Jamup and Honey," I begged. "They'll be on any minute."

Mama laid down the law. "We'll stay 10 more minutes and not a second more."

We all thought Jamup and Honey were black people, when actually they were two white men, Bunny Biggs and Lee Davis Wilds, in black faces and fake accents.

"Make way, folks," the Solemn Ole Judge announced, "fer ever'body's favorite comedians, Jamup and Honey."

When the applause died down, we heard Honey call sleepily, "Jamup, Ah hears somethin' comin in the house."

Jamup: "See whut it is and let me git some shuteye. May jist be yer ole hound dawg."

Honey: "I think hit's in the room with us. I kin hyar hit breathin'. Now whar's my shotgun? I blow hit to smithereens."

Boom!

Honey: "*Yeoh! Yeoh!* Oh, me! Oh, my! Jamup, blood is runnin' down ma foot. Ohhhhh, ohhhhh. I think I've kilt maself. Strike up a light."

We heard the scratch of a match.

Jamup: "Naw, ye ain't. Ye've jist shot off yer big toe."

When the laughing died down, Mama went for the babies. Daddy lit the lantern and handed it to Grampa Tom. We left Grampa at his house; then I took the lantern and we trudged up the hill to our place. I fell asleep in my loft bed as I dreamed of going to Nashville to see the Grand Ole Opry.

Keep Watching the Ozarks

Two years later we got our own radio, a Silvertone shelf model with a battery bigger than the cabinet. The Opry remained the big event of the week. On other evenings we listened to "Korn's-a-Crackin'" from Ralph Foster's KWTO— Keep Watching the Ozarks—in Springfield, MO. I sang along with Slim Pickens Wilson, who had been plucked out of an Ozark cornfield to perform on KWTO.

Now I like grits and gravy,
I like ham and beans;
Nothing hit the spot for me
Like cabbage greens.
Bile them cabbage down,
And turn 'em round and 'round.
Stop that foolin', Mary Jane,

And bile them cabbage down.

Korns-a-Crackin' evolved into the Ozark Jubilee with Ernest Tubb, Red Foley, Hawkshaw Hawkins, Tex Ritter, and others who later moved on to the Grand Old Opry. We loved them all.

Grampa's Kind of Music

Some nights we gathered at Grampa Tom's house for an evening of our own music. Grampa perched in his hickory-bottom chair, fiddle tucked under his chin, black cat bouncing on his knee, warming us up with *Sally Good'un.* We closed the show with a gospel song, with Grampa accompanying on the fiddle and Daddy on the guitar.

In June 1937 Grampa was attending a Country singing school when he fell to the floor. He had suffered a stroke. "Take 'em back to his own house." Doc Sexton told his sons. Daddy and my uncles took Grampa home in a spring wagon.

Grampa lay in bed unable to talk or to play his fiddle. His black cat snoozed beside him. Now and then he would awaken, look over at his cat and fiddle, make funny noises and cry. Uncle Loma — Daddy's younger brother — and Aunt Clara lived with him. Grampa had 11 children, so family members visited him almost every evening. Daddy played the guitar, Cousin Athel the fiddle, and Grampa rubbed a rough hand across his fiddle strings, made noises, and cried.

Grampa Tom now had his own radio. Many a Saturday night we sat around his bed and listened with him to the Grand Ole Opry. He'd mouth the words with Roy Acuff singing *The Great Speckled Bird* and *The Wabash Cannonball.* He'd twitch his feet a little when Uncle Dave Macon played the fiddle. Then he'd stroke his cat and his fiddle and cry.

One wintry evening after supper at Grampa's house we

walked into the front room to be near the fire. Daddy began twanging on his guitar. Somebody struck up a Country gospel tune,

Now let us have a little talk with Jesus,
Let us tell 'em all about air troubles,
He will hyar air faintest cry . . . and
He will answer by and by.

Sounds—words!—emerged from the bed. "Pa's a sangin' with us!" Daddy shouted in amazement. Sure enough, he was. But when the song stopped, Grampa lay like he was a mouse in a trap. He was still moving his lips but was unable to talk.

Grampa died in 1939. His sons carried him in a pine coffin to the family graveyard above our house. Preacher Dan Hefley delivered a short sermon that was punctuated by "Hallelujahs" and then led us in a gospel song which everybody knew by heart. I'd heard it many times on the Grand Ole Opry:

O they tell me of a home far beyond the skies,
O they tell me of a land far away,
O they tell me that He smiles on His children thar,
O the land of the unclouded day.

That year I completed the eighth grade in the one-room White House school a mile down the creek from our house.

"You're goin' to high school," Mama said. She and Daddy bought a "jot-'em-down" store in the little town of Mount Judy (Judea, if you want to sound like a "furriner"), five miles down the creek. On many a Saturday afternoon Daddy, Cousin Athel, and other musicians gathered around the pot-bellied stove and entertained customers with Country songs and tunes. Daddy sang about a "derned ole billygoat" who grabbed the clothes off Mama's line and "flagged down that derned ole freight [train]." I never heard that song on the Grand Old Opry. Daddy may have made it up or got it from Grampa. I never thought to ask Daddy before he died.

Mama didn't care for Cousin Athel's favorite:

Down the road here from me
There's an old holler tree,
Where you lay down a dollar 'er two.
Then you go around the bend,
And when you come back ag'in,
There's jug full
Of good ole mountain dew.

Men and boys whooped and patted their feet to the rhythm. When Cousin Athel stopped, Mama delivered her sermon. "Boys, I call it that bad ole mountain dew. Even if they do sing it on the Grand Ole Opry."

I left home as the first among 60-some first cousins to attend college. God called me into the ministry. (You can read about that in my book, *Way Back in the Hills.*) While I attended seminary in New Orleans, I met Marti Smedley, a Michigan import who said she listened to the Grand Opera every Saturday.

"Me, too," I noted.

We had different "operas" in mind. She meant the Metropolitan Grand Opera of New York City. But our differences in musical taste didn't keep us from loving each other. We've celebrated 40 years of marriage.

A Dream Becomes Reality

After eight years as a pastor in New Orleans and two years as an editor in Elgin IL, I became a full-time freelance writer. Finally I got a book assignment in Nashville to assist Jimmie Snow in writing his autobiography. Jimmie lived—and still does—next to his famous father, Hank Snow.

One Saturday night my dream became reality and even more. Jimmie took me backstage at the Grand Ole Opry. I saw Minnie Pearl putting on her flowered hat to go on stage and Roy Acuff peeping out of dressing room Number One. I caught sight of a plaque behind Roy:

THERE AIN'T NUTHIN' GONNA COME UP TODAY THAT ME AND THE LORD CAN'T HANDLE.

A few minutes later I stood just a few feet behind Roy and his Smoky Mountain Boys as he belted out *The Wabash Cannonball*. One of the biggest dreams of my childhood had been realized.

Jimmie Snow's autobiography led to a book on Country music. Marti and I were living in Chattanooga, TN, then—just a two-hour hop up I-24 to the Country-music capital of the world. I spent many a Friday and Saturday night backstage at the Opry as I interviewed stars for my book.

I soon learned that Roy, Minnie Pearl, Hank Snow, and other "traditionalists" were seen as back numbers in the new Country music corral. Big money from Hollywood and New York had moved into Nashville. Family and fidelity in marriage were out. Loose sex was in. Paul Harvey put it this way: "Historically, Country music reflected apple pie, patriotism, virtue, boy-girl romance. Much of today's pottage is downright porno."

I sampled some of the recent hits and decided Harvey was on target:

Ronnie McDowell was asking *How Far Do You Want to Go?* Dollie Parton was comparing her body to a *Bargain Store*. Larry Gatlin was willing to *Walk a Mile to Love Sweet Becky Walker.*

Glen Campbell was crooning *When You're Lying Next to Me, Just Love Me Every Which Way You Can, Let's Git It While the Gittin's Good*, and *She Was Wild and She Was Willing*.

As Don Williams sang, "I don't believe virginity is as common as it used to be."

My book, *How Sweet the Sound*, was published by Tyndale House in 1980. The "new sound" rolled on and brought in megabucks for artists who didn't mind singing the gutter tunes that the "new morality" moguls wanted. Definitely not what we were hearing at our Hefley Family Reunion held in Mt. Judy every even-numbered year on the Saturday before Labor Day. At these get-togethers my now "silver-haired daddy" and cousins sang the old songs. The 300 to 400 folks who were there enjoyed them all.

In 1988 Daddy attended his last reunion. He and his performing partner Greg Cantrell, sang *Canaan's Jubilee* and *Salvation's Been Brought Down*. That evening Daddy suffered a heart attack and joined Mama, who had departed for the heavenly Canaan four years before.

Amazing Branson

Marti and I moved to Mark Twain's hometown of Hannibal, MO. For Hefley family get-togethers this meant driving south through Springfield and Branson and on into Arkansas.

On every trip down US 65 the traffic approaching Branson got worse. Where were all of these people going? To the new "Country-music capital of the world", I was told, With my loyalty to Nashville I wasn't ready to accept that, even though Branson was in my neck of the woods.

My immediate family gathers for mini-reunions during odd-numbered years. In 1991 we decided to hold the get-together in Branson. My sisters made reservations at a motel a mile west on Highway 76 from the junction with 65. I drove down Friday afternoon and turned onto the 76 "Strip" into bumper-to-bumper, inch-along traffic. I spent 45 minutes trying to reach the motel—a mile in three-quarters of an hour! I could have crawled faster than that.

Stories about the new Country-music center now were appearing in national magazines. "Welcome to Branson, MO (pop 3,706)" said *Time* in a business piece titled "Country Music's New Mecca." Noted *Time*, "This hardscrabble town attracts five million tourists a year, who drop an estimated $1.5 billion into local pockets."

I began listening to Country-music radio again. My ears perked up. Here was Randy Travis rhapsodizing on *Forever and Ever, Amen*, which had risen to Number One on the charts. It was a song about a couple staying together in marriage into of looking for "love" in a honkytonk.

And here was Glen Campbell, the old "Rhinestone Cowboy" starring in the Grand Palace, Branson's answer to Nashville's Opry House, singing *No More Night* about Jesus delivering him from drugs and alcohol.

I stopped on one journey down to see the home folks and visited with Jay Scribner, pastor of the First Baptist Church of Branson. "Branson's just a good, clean, wholesome entertainment center," Jay said. "It's Las Vegas without gambling and nudity."

I went back to Nashville and talked with friends in the industry there. Billy Walker, on the Opry for more than 30 years, told me, "Country music in Branson and also in Nashville has moral values. It's the TV and movie entertainment out of L.A. and New York that's dirty and rotten and no good. Dan Quayle was right about that."

I set to work on this book. I wanted to fuse the past to the present and tell about Country-music personalities who have played leading roles in bringing much of Country music full-circle back home to where it began. Read on and see if you don't think Country music is really "comin' home."

Chapter 2
Rooted in Faith and Family

Preacher Dan Hefley's long-legged, guitar-picking, gospel-singing daughters never made it to the Grand Ole Opry. They started in the annual fall brush-arbor revival in a cleared spot in the woods, two miles down the creek from Grampa Tom's house. While his daughters picked and sang, Uncle Dan danced to the rhythm and shouted, "Glory! Glory! I feel happy tonight, folks! Come, jine in the singin'." Perched high in a white-oak tree, I watched the goings-on with puzzled interest.

Uncle Dan was a Pentecostal—a "Holy Roller", some called him. He had a ready answer for people who said guitars and fiddles didn't belong in a church service: "Genesis 4:21, folks. Hit's right thar in yer Bible. Ole Jubal, the seventh generation from Adam, was the father of instrumental music. I expect ole Adam did some sangin' 'fore then."

Uncle Dan had it right. Music's as old as humankind. Men and women from Adam to Noah sang. They sang from Abraham to Queen Elizabeth. Shakespeare's tales are filled with songs and dances, as in this little verse from Act III of *Henry the Eighth:*

Everything that heard him play,
Even the billows of the sea,
Hung their heads and then lay by;

In sweet music is such art;
Killing care and grief of heart
Fall asleep, or, hearing die.

"The man that hath no music in himself," the old Bard wrote in *Merchant of Venice*, "is fit for treasons, strategems, and spoils."

European colonists brought to America their folk songs and ballads, be they sad or joyful. Tear-puddling *Barbara Allen*, for example, hailed straight from Scotland. They sang it in Virginia, the Carolinas, Georgia, and Texas—as one wit remarked, "before the pale faces were thick enough to make the Indians consider a massacre worthwhile."

The American pioneers sang to the accompaniment of stringed instruments. Some of their songs were *Froggie Went-A-Courtin', My Luv's Like a Red, Red Rose, Can She Bake a Cherry Pie?*, and many other wholesome ditties in the valleys and on the mountains, at church socials and square-dancing frolics.

Country Music Goes on Records

In 1877 Thomas A. Edison gave birth to the recording industry. His first record was only a small metal cylinder wrapped in tin foil and mounted on an axle that could be rotated. He attached a mouthpiece with a vibrating disk next to the cylinder. When someone spoke into the mouthpiece, the cylinder was turned. The sound waves made the disk and needle vibrate. This made small dents in the tin foil—the first sound waves ever captured by a human being. Edison mouthed the first words ever put on record:

Mary had a little lamb;
Its fleece was white as snow.
Everywhere that Mary went
The lamb was sure to go.

While the miracle of recording developed, Country music, as it ultimately was called, rang through rural and small-town Southern Appalachia—the Virginias, Tennessee, the Carolinas, Kentucky, Arkansas, Georgia—the delta South, and across the Western plains and mountains. The songs ranged from the funeral favorite, *Will the Circle Be Unbroken?*, to ballads of tragedy such as *The Sinking of the Titanic*; from earthy ditties such as *Who Bit the Wart off Grandma's Nose?* to the fast rhythm of fiddle classics such as *Turkey in the Straw*; from the cowboy favorite, *Go On, You Little Doggies*, to the love lyrics of *My Love Is a Rider*. The songs reflected the beliefs of the people: Life is tough but sometimes funny; love is sweet and parting bitter; death is certain and often tragic; God is real and heaven everlasting.

Through it all, the strong, life-sustaining faith of the people ran like an unbroken thread. Dr. Bill Malone, Country music's greatest historian, says the country knew "no greater influence on Country music than Southern religious life, both as to the nature of the songs and to the manner in which they were performed."

By the time I was a youngster, Edison's device had a flat record instead of a cylinder and was called a gramophone. The Kents had the first one in upper Big Creek Valley. I stood in awe and listened to pioneers Ernest and Hattie Stoneman sing *The Sinking of the Titanic* as the needle followed the record 'round and 'round. I could almost hear the people screaming and see the "unsinkable" ship going down.

The Singing Stonemans

Few Country-music records were made before 1924. That year Ernest "Pop" Stoneman was working in a mill in Bluefield, WV, when he heard Henry Wittier singing on a record. Pop wrote Columbia and Okeh Records in New York: "Give me a chance, and I'll do better."

Both companies offered auditions if Pop would travel to New York. All summer he saved his wages and then made the trip. During the next four years Pop and Hattie Stoneman recorded more than 200 songs. Their biggest number, *The Sinking of the Titanic*, sold more than a million copies, but they earned only a few hundred dollars from it.

The Stonemans are reckoned among the founders of commercial Country music. Born in 1893 Pop was reared in a log cabin in the Blue Ridge Mountains of Virginia. At a church he met Hattie Frost and for seven years courted her. He walked an accumulative 5,200 miles between his house and hers. Hattie gave birth to 23 children (including five sets of twins), of which 15 survived.

"My folks weren't Catholics, just passionate Baptists," jokes daughter Ronnie on *Hee-Haw*.

As each child got old enough to hold an instrument, Pop would tune an instrument he had made, leave it on a bed, and warn the child, "Don't you touch this while I'm gone." Soon he had enough Stonemans for three hillbilly bands.

A bachelor had a tough-enough job in the '30s keeping body and soul together, much less a family the size of the Stonemans. But Pop took carpentry jobs only when absolutely necessary. Music was the love of his life; he was determined to succeed.

Son Eddie remembers cutting grass for neighbors just so he could use their bathtub when the Stonemans lived in an old

Virginia farmhouse outside Washington, DC. After they moved to Maryland, Pop built a one-room shack with a canvas roof. At times the children had to solicit food at fire and police stations. Once in school daughter Patsy fainted from hunger.

Pop and Eddie played and sang for Arthur Godfrey's radio show in 1935. That brought in a few jobs paying from $1.50 to $10 a performance. They sang gospel songs on a radio station and got stacks of fan mail. When the station owner couldn't pay them a living wage, the Stonemans went off the air.

"Pop would go anywhere to get the family on stage," son Dean recalls. "We were always in trouble with school boards."

Finally after World War II they were invited to perform in Washington's Constitution Hall. The show was telecast, but the children were unaware of the cameras. Donna returned home from school and told Ronnie a classmate had seen them on television. "What's television?"

In the 1950s their fortune turned upward. Pop won $20,000 on a TV quiz show. Son Scott won the annual National Fiddling Championship seven times. Part of the family took first place on Arthur Godfrey's "Talent Show."

The Stonemans moved to Nashville to sing on the Grand Ole Opry. In the 1960s they secured sponsors for their own nationally syndicated TV show, "Those Stonemans." In 1967 the Country Music Association voted them "Vocal Group of the Year." Then in 1979 nine Stoneman children performed at the Museum of Natural History in Washington in recognition of the pioneer role their family had played in Country music.

Pop Stoneman died in 1968 at age 75; Hattie passed away in 1976. The children and grandchildren still hold a family reunion every August on Sand Mountain, AL. Hundreds of fans travel there to hear them sing the old hymns and ballads and do the comedy routines developed by Pop Stoneman.

The Carter Family Dynasty

More influential than the Stonemans was the legendary
Carter family–Doc, Sara, and Maybelle—all devout Christians.

From Stoneman country to Carter country in Virginia is
less than 75 miles as the crow flies. One of nine children, Doc
(Alvin Pleasant) Carter was born in 1891 in a log cabin just a
few miles from the Cumberland Gap. A tall, lean, jug-eared,
long-nosed hillbilly, Doc played the guitar and fiddle and sold
fruit trees around the area.

One selling trip took him over a mountain to the Copper
Creek settlement. Always on the lookout for other musicians
Doc met a dark-haired, black-eyed, talented mountain girl.
Sara Dougherty played the autoharp, banjo, and guitar and
sang the old ballads and hymns with a voice as clear as a cow
bell on a frosty morning. Doc was 24 and Sara 15 when they
married.

The third member of the musical Carters arrived 11 years
later when Sara's comely cousin Maybelle married Doc's
brother, Ezra. A trio was formed with Sara singing lead,
Maybelle alto, and Doc bass. Ezra farmed and kept them eating.

Doc already had been leading the choir at the Friendly
Grove Methodist Church. He and the two cousins sang there as
well as at other churches and for various social events in the
area. Doc thought the group was pretty good and got excited
on learning that Ralph Peer of the Victor Talking Machine
Company would be in Bristol, VA, to record Country musicians.

The announcement Doc saw noted that the Stonemans
would be recording for $100 a day. A hundred dollars for
singing a few songs sounded almost too good to be true.

Doc and Sara now had two children. His parents believed

the time had arrived for him to settle down and sell fruit trees or at least farm. Maybelle was in her seventh month of pregnancy with her first child. Ezra didn't want her traveling the 25 miles to Bristol over rough roads. But Doc was determined and offered to clear a field of weeds for Ezra if he'd let Maybelle make the trip. Ezra finally gave in; they loaded their instruments into Doc's Model A and started for Bristol.

The Stonemans had already arrived and left when the Carters arrived in late July 1927. Doc, Sara, and Maybelle got in line with scores of other aspiring Country musicians who had arrived by bus, horse and buggy, car, train, and on foot. They waited their turn to record in the rug-draped studio on the second floor of an old warehouse. When Ralph Peer heard the Carters' clear, natural voices, he immediately recognized talent. On three records he recorded *Bury Me Under the Weeping Willow*, *Poor Orphan Child*, and four other Carter Family songs.

The Carters' eyes widened when Peer handed $300 in advance money on record royalties for the three songs. They left for home in triumph.

The "Blue Yodeler"

Two days later, a skinny, sickly yodeler named Jimmie Rodgers showed up in Bristol. A railroad brakeman from Meridian, MS, the aspiring performer had been singing on the road in North Carolina when he was told of Peer's invitation.

The "Singing Brakeman", also called the "Blue Yodeler", was quite the opposite of the moral, deeply religious, family oriented Carters. His mother had died when he was 6; he had been bandied among relatives. At 13 he ran away with a medicine show. When this job ran out, he worked on the railroad and from black section hands learned blues songs as well as guitar and banjo-playing.

He married Stella McWilliams but couldn't support her and their daughter, Kathryn. Stella finally took the child to her parents' home.

Without waiting for a divorce Jimmie began courting Carrie Williamson, the 16-year-old daughter of a Methodist preacher. He promised her daddy that he would attend church. He went at least once. When the divorce became legal, he and Carrie eloped and broke her family's heart. Carrie couldn't reform him either. As fast as he made it, he spent money on women and liquor. "I want to live," he'd say. "You wait, Carrie. Someday I'll amount to something."

Carrie must have known that he had a girl in every town where he made music. Still she stuck with him and bore a daughter, Anita, in 1921. A second daughter, June, was born two years later and died soon after birth. Jimmie was away and had to pawn his banjo to get back for the baby's funeral.

When the "Blue Yodeler" arrived in Bristol, he already knew he had tuberculosis and probably just a few years to live. He coughed and wheezed and had difficulty recording. Peer got only two songs from him—*The Soldier's Sweetheart* and a lullaby, *Sleep, Baby, Sleep.*

Five weeks later Jimmie took the train to New York City and registered at an expensive hotel. He brashly told the clerk that the Victor Company would pay the bill. He then rang up Ralph Peer to say he was in town for recordings.

Within six months the sickly, blues-singing yodeler was earning $2,000 per month. Most of his songs were written by his first wife's sister, Elsie McWilliams. Her only previous writing experience had been in preparing Bible studies for her church.

Looking for Songs

Meanwhile Doc Carter was scouring Virginia for songs. Coaxing his Model A over rough roads and often having to walk to more remote settlements, he asked everyone he met to "tell me the old songs your family loves best."

Doc didn't worry about authorship and made any changes that he thought would improve a song. He never realized that, more than anyone else, he was building a repository of music that would preserve traditional ballads and would provide a foundation for a multi-million-dollar industry.

Between song-hunting excursions Doc, Sara, and Maybelle performed in towns around the region. Doc advertised their show with handbills:

LOOK
VICTOR ARTIST A.P. CARTER
AND THE CARTER FAMILY
WILL GIVE A MUSICAL PROGRAM
AT _____
ON _____
COME ONE AND ALL
ADMISSION 15 CENTS AND 35 CENTS.

The "Brakeman's" Last Ride

While the Carters stayed closer to home, Jimmie Rodgers performed in large cities. His income soared to $100,000 a year, a stupendous sum during the early years of the Great Depression. Younger and healthier singers already were imitating both his yodeling and lonesome style.

Carter records also sold well. The Carters' hymns and mountain ballads and Jimmie Rodgers' lonesome blues were played on Victrolas from Maine to California. Among rural people the Carters and Stonemans and Jimmie Rodgers got to be as well-known as President Herbert Hoover.

In 1931 Ralph Peer brought Jimmie and the Carters together for recording sessions in Louisville. Now in intense pain Jimmie left a trail of blood from coughing spasms and could not stay on stage for more than 20 minutes at a time. He was making more money than President Hoover, yet he refused to slow down. Doctors warned him that he was shortening his life with cigarettes and alcohol, but he refused to give up either.

In Louisville Jimmie cut a hymn, *The Wonderful City*, written by Elsie McWilliams. He was so weak that Maybelle Carter had to play his guitar while he sang.

The Singing Brakeman was headed for the final downgrade. Hat still cocked jauntily on his head, he looked as though he was a walking dead man when he sauntered on stage. Between recordings he often had to rest on a cot. His first wife was suing him for child support for his teen-aged daughter. Stories were spreading that his patient second wife, Carrie, was about to leave him.

In May 1933 he was in New York cutting more records. A matronly nurse was looking after him in a hotel. On the evening of the 25th she stopped outside his room. Hearing a fit of coughing she checked and found him hemorrhaging. Since he'd already been bleeding frequently, she waited until the bleeding stopped and then went to her room.

Just before midnight she returned to find him hemorrhaging again. Before she could get him to a hospital, the famous Blue Yodeler fell into a coma and drowned in his own blood. The "father" of modern honky-tonk music and the first person to be installed into the Country Music Hall of Fame was dead at 35.

Jimmie Rodgers' body was put on a special car and taken

by train to Meridian. Hundreds waited at the railroad station where he had hung out as a boy. Late in the night they heard the low, funereal moan of the engine's whistle, the sound Jimmie had learned to mimic so well. Then the train pulled into the station and the hometown folk surged forward to see his coffin. He had shown them; he'd become a star.

The Blue Yodeler was buried in a country cemetery beside his baby daughter, June. Hearing of his death, his first wife, Stella, sat through the night playing his records over and over. Several years later his oldest daughter, Kathryn, swallowed a fatal dose of disinfectant.

"Keep on the Sunny Side"

Doc and Sara Carter now were having marital problems. Doc had kept up with the career of Jimmie Rodgers and was eager to launch out into the big cities. Sara wanted to spend more time at home with their family. They had two daughters and were expecting a third child. When Doc would not give up his musical ambitions, Sara took the children and went back to her relatives. Three years later she got a divorce, a rare and shocking thing then in southwest Virginia.

That same year the Carters signed a contract with the notorious "Dr." John R. Brinkley to sing on the powerful border station, XER. Brinkley had paid the Mexican government for the right to build across from Del Rio, TX. Sara took the children to Texas but refused to be reconciled with Doc. Maybelle's husband, Ezra, traveled down as soon as he could leave his railroad job.

Before moving across the Mexican border Brinkley had broadcast from his own station in Kansas, where he had the largest radio audience in the country. He employed Country musicians and sold by mail an extract from goat glands which

27

he claimed would cure sexual impotency. When the U.S. government lifted his license for the quackery, he moved to Mexico.

In good weather the 250,000-watt XER could be heard in every state in the U.S. It blasted over the signals of American stations which were limited to 50,000 watts. Brinkley paid the Carters only $75 a week but gave them six-months vacation a year. He could afford to be generous. Appearing every evening except Sunday, the Carters drew an audience of millions with their best-loved hymns and ballads. Between numbers Brinkley hawked Kolor Bak and other patent remedies. The cream for the Carters occurred with spiraling record sales.

The Carters were like neighbors to us in Big Creek Valley. If we were visiting at Grampa Tom's, at the Kents, or at home, everything stopped when the Carters' theme song, *Keep on the Sunny Side*, hit the airways. Fifty years later I can still remember the tune and many of the words. In the dreary Depression years of the 1930s the Carters brought sunshine into our lives. More than one mountain woman stopped Uncle Elmer Hefley, who brought our mail by horseback, to give him egg money for a money order to send off for a bottle of "that thar Kolor Bak which they're talkin' about on the Carter Family's program."

Doc Carter still managed the group. As religious as ever he now was giving 70 percent of his money to Christian causes. Any hopes he had of winning Sara back were dashed when she went home and married his cousin, Coy Bayes. The wedding took place in their home church, Mount Vernon Methodist. Ezra Carter was best man and Maybelle maid of honor. Doc watched sadly from the back of the church.

The clan returned to Texas the next day for one more season. Maybelle and Ezra's daughters, June, Helen, and Anita, began performing.

In 1940 they moved to WBT, Charlotte, NC. Three years later the original Carter Family disbanded. Sara and her second husband, Coy Bayes, left for California. Maybelle and her three daughters performed in Richmond, VA, for a while and then joined Ralph Foster's Ozark Jamboree at KWTO in Springfield, MO.

On the way to Springfield they stopped in Nashville and picked up a starving young guitar player. They took him to Missouri for his send-off to fame. Chet Atkins would become the most acclaimed guitarist in the industry.

Ezra Carter was also with them—he'd quit his railroad job to manage the career of wife Maybelle and daughters. Doc, who had started the original Carter family, remained in Virginia, where he ran a general store and filled his lonely hours with church work.

Headquartered with the Ozark Jubilee, "Mother Maybelle and the Carter Sisters", as they were billed, toured for a few months with a super-polite, young Pentecostal singer named Elvis Presley. In 1950 Maybelle, Ezra, and their girls returned to Nashville and joined the Grand Ole Opry, while Elvis starred in movies and rocked to stardom with the newest music craze.

Mother Maybelle and her daughter remained with the Opry for 17 years. When the children went their separate ways, Maybelle sang at folk festivals. She appeared with Woody Guthrie and Bob Dylan. June Carter became an actress and appeared on "Jim Bowie" and "Gunsmoke." After her marriage to musician Carl Smith failed, she returned to work with her mother and sisters.

Newly reunited, "Mother Maybelle and the Carter Sisters" toured with celebrated Johnny Cash, whom they had met while they worked with Elvis. Johnny's own marriage was on the rocks; he was battling with drugs. Maybelle and Ezra, who still had a strong marriage, tried to help him. June was concerned, too, for she was in love with the husky, deep-throated singer from Dyess, AR.

In 1969 Doc Carter died a lonely and disappointed man. He was buried in the graveyard of the Mount Vernon Methodist Church. A gold record, sculpted on his rose marble gravestone, bore the simple inscription:

A.P. CARTER
KEEP ON THE SUNNY SIDE

Sara Carter Bayes died in 1971. Johnny Cash sang one of her favorite hymns, *Farther Along,* at her funeral. She was buried in the Mount Vernon cemetery just down the hill from Doc's plot. Ezra died in 1975.

A Blessed Heritage

Mother Maybelle followed in 1978 and was given one of th biggest funerals in Nashville history. The service began with a slow piano version of *The Wabash Cannonball.* Tom T. Hall sang *Keep on the Sunny Side,* while the audience clapped in rhythm. Chet Atkins strummed Maybelle's most famous guitar number, *Wildwood Flower.* Jan Howard sang *No One Stands Alone.*

Johnny Cash in his trademark black suit and white ruffled shirt delivered a short eulogy and read tributes from President Jimmy Carter, evangelist Billy Graham, and others. Looking down at the bronze coffin and with a voice choked with emotion Johnny said, "Here lies the shell of Maybelle Carter. But her soul lives forever. She was my friend, fellow worker, mother-in-law (Johnny was now married to June Carter), and fishing buddy. She was a good Christian. I never heard Mother speak an unkind word in he 18 years I knew her."

As they filed by her coffin, friends and relatives sang, "May the Circle Be Unbroken."

Mother Maybelle's death ended an era in Country music. Said E.W. "Bud" Wendell, general manager of The Grand Ole Opry: "The influence of the Carters is so great, it can't be measured. Every Country music performer owes something to this family."

One of the finest tributes was panned by Gene Thorpe of the *Atlanta Journal*: "The Carters' music compares to today's Country music as a virgin compares to a prostitute . . . The Carters sang of life's verities; today's singers sing of some girl trembling as she drops her gown to the floor . . . The Carters' songs are timeless."

Country Singers Who Started in Church

The songs of the Carters, the Stonemans, and to some extent those of Jimmie Rogers had their deepest roots in the Bible-Belt culture of rural and small-town Southern America. So did many in the generations of Country artists who followed them.

"Most of us grew up around churches and small-town congregations," says Bill Anderson, member of the Grand Ole Opry since 1962 and star of his own TV show. "I don't believe there are a half-dozen persons on the Opry who didn't start out by singing in a church choir, singing religious songs, or maybe singing in a family unit that traveled as a religious group."

Anderson doesn't fit the stereotype of the Hee-Haw hillbilly. A former deejay and graduate in journalism from the University of Georgia, he acknowledges the influence of his grandfather, a Methodist preacher.

Roy Acuff—now pushing 90—and his Smoky Mountain Boys auditioned for the Opry on September 15, 1938. At that audition Roy introduced *The Great Speckled Bird. The Bird,* as it is called today, led to his first recording contract.

Roy's preacher father made an impact on his life when Roy as very young. "I was raised by the Bible in a Christian family," says the "King of Country Music", the title friend Dizzy Dean gave him. "I went to the Baptist Young People's Union and Sunday school, hardly missing a Sunday before coming to Nashville and going on the road as a musician."

Reverend Neil Acuff, Roy's father, once pastor of the Fountain City Baptist Church near Knoxville, TN, practiced law and also served as an elected judge. When Roy began carousing during his teen years, his father urged him to return to the straight and narrow. "You're going to be a leader," he predicted. "You've got to live up to that responsibility." Roy never forgot that admonition.

Thousands now journey to Nashville just to hear Roy sing *The Bird* and *The Wabash Cannonball*, his two biggest songs, and to watch him yo-yo and balance his fiddle bow on his nose. Roy Acuff truly is the "king" of today's Country music.

If Roy Acuff is the king, then Johnny Carter is the swashbuckling crown prince. I've saved the story of his dramatic turnaround from drinking, womanizing, and pill-popping for a later chapter in this book. As a boy back in Arkansas and before he went astray, he never missed Baptist church services Sunday morning and night and on Wednesday evening. Johnny's paternal grandfather led singing in a Methodist church for 40 years. Johnny's father was a deacon and Sunday-school teacher.

Wilma Lee Cooper, another old-time Country great, wife of the late Stoney Cooper, developed a repertoire of gospel songs from singing with her Leary family beside the pump organ at home. The Learys provided inspiration for church services, comfort at funerals, and entertainment at community social events.

Willie Nelson grew up in a Methodist church in Texas and sang in the choir. "I learned to love gospel songs and still do," Willie says. After his parents divorced, Willie's mother wanted him to have a Christian upbringing. She left him and his sister, Bobbi, with their devout grandmother. Willie's grandmother penned gospel songs. At an early age Willie himself began writing them.

Other Country Greats with Gospel Roots

When he was age 6, Larry Gatlin began singing gospel songs in Texas with his two younger brothers, Steve and Rudy. Their mother was the pianist; they later were joined in the choir by their younger sister, LaDonna. "God meant for me to write and sing with my family," Larry says, "not just to entertain but to move and touch people."

The one and only Dolly Parton grew up in the Church of God in Sevierville, TN. "It was a very free church," she remembers. "If anybody wanted to get up and sing or shout his feelings, he could do it." Her grandfather, the Reverend Jake Owens, pastor of the church for many years, was the model for her song, "Old-Time Preacher Man." Dolly, who has been given the honorary doctor of letters degree by Tennessee's Carson-Newman Baptist College, says that when she's home "and they're having a revival, I go and sing as I used to do when I was a girl back there."

As a boy Hank Williams sat on the piano bench beside his mother while she played the piano for services of their church in Alabama. Many years later Hank became famous for his trademark religious song, *I Saw the Light*.

Roy Drusky, who has had more than 50 records on the charts, sang in the youth choir at Moreland Baptist Church in Georgia. His mother was church pianist.

Ronnie Millsap, born in the hills near Robinsonville, NC, also "sang in the church and enjoyed the gospel songs that were so much a part of my heritage."

Hank Snow, who named his only son for Jimmie Rodgers, gave his first performance in a Canadian church hall.

Conway Twitty not only sang in churches, he also preached for two-and-a-half years during his teens. When he heard some church leaders were deceiving people, he reportedly became disillusioned and quit the pulpit but not music.

Gene Autry sang his first solo in the Indian Creek Baptist church in Tioga, TX. His grandfather, the Reverend William Autry, was the pastor.

Jeannie C. Riley of *Harper Valley PTA* fame cherishes "Precious Memories" of a grandfather who preached for 50 years. She, too, sang at church and at school functions.

Bobbie Gentry, best known for her *Ode to Billy Jo*e, was reared on a farm with her grandparents in Chickasaw County, MS. She wrote her first song before she was 7-years old. "The church was terribly important to us. There I learned my music," she recalls. "I taught myself to play by watching Ginny Sue, the pianist at the Pleasant Grove Baptist Church."

Connie Smith, who has sung at the Presidential Prayer Breakfast, also was reared in church.

So was George Hamilton IV, the most popular American Country music star in Europe.

Jeannie Pruett says she sings *The Old Rugged Cross* just as she did back home in Alabama.

George Jones' mother was a church pianist.

The Wilburn Brothers got their start singing in churches and schoolhouses in the Arkansas and Missouri Ozarks.

Tom T. Hall, the "Storyteller of Country Music", is one of eight children from a Kentucky Appalachian family. His father was a minister in Olive Hill, KY.

The popular Hagar Brothers duo on *Hee-Haw* hailed from a preacher's home in Illinois.

Having roots in churches has helped develop many singing careers. Teddy Wilburn, who says he was spiritually reborn in 1976, puts things this way: "A lot of performers cut their teeth on Christian music and were raised in churches. But that doesn't mean they're Christians. Singing about God and the Bible and knowing the cliches of religion are not enough. You've got to have a personal relationship with God."

Chapter 3
Take 'Er Away, Boys

Before the Branson boom Nashville was the undisputed capital of Country music.

Nashville was founded on Christmas Day 1779 when James Robertson and his shivering band of pioneers crossed the Cumberland River and began building Fort Nashborough on a bluff. The city, named for a Revolutionary War hero, now has a metro population of nearly half a million. people.

Nashville leads the world in religious publishing and is renowned as an intellectual center. A replica of the Greek Parthenon stands near the Vanderbilt University campus. Meharry College and Medical School has graduated almost half of the nation's black doctors. Tennessee State University, home of the famous Tigerbelles, the women's track team, has sent more athletes to the Olympics than any other school in the world has.

But the city is best-known worldwide for Country music and the Grand Ole Opry. Some of the "Vanderbilt set" once looked down their cultured noses at "that bunch of hillbillies" performing on Saturday nights, Not any more. Ninety-five percent of all Country-music recordings are made in Nashville, which is the world center for contemporary gospel and quartet music. By Jimmie Snow's last count Nashville has 317 recording studios. Around 300 music publishers are there. They are making sure that everybody gets his cut from sales and airplay.

Down on Music Row

The "heart" of the Country-music industry is Music Row, an uneven gaggle of modernistic edifices and converted residences strung along several blocks of 16th and 17th Streets on the south side of I-40 from downtown Nashville. Here are stabled the production firms, booking agencies, songwriters, agents, publicists, and publishers that turn the wheels of the industry.

The business executives don't all wear suits and ties. The stars are more likely to arrive in tailored jeans and Western shirts. Walk around a little; you might see a familiar artist climbing from a chauffeured Cadillac or Continental en route to a recording session. You also night spot a "good ole boy or girl" fresh from Hickory Crossroads or some other unknown place as they pack a guitar and a bag of demo tapes and move from one studio to another trying to sweet talk their way past secretaries. You might even hear someone humming Dolly Parton's *Down on Music Row*. "If you want to be a star, that's where you've got to go."

At the head of Music Row stands the glittering Country Music Hall of Fame Museum, where the tour buses move in to disgorge fans who arrive to gaze at the immortalized faces of the dead and living and their awards, instruments, and costumes from other days. Johnny Cash's section, for example, includes report cards and diplomas from Dyess (Arkansas) High School, where Johnny got at least one "A" in conduct. You'll also see a written statement from a grown-up Johnny: "God is the strength of my being. He gave me all I have." And another line from the Man in Black: "People are looking for realism and truth in music. That's why Country music is the best."

Slapped on the wall is a big promo-pix of Loretta Lynn, the *Coal Miner's Daughter*—"married at thirteen, four kids by twenty. She's been hungry and poor. She's been loved and cheated on. She became a singer because it was the only thing she could do. She became a star because it was the only way she could do it."

That manly voice you hear is Ernest Tubbs, *Walking the Floor* over You. Those shoes you see are the Duke of Paducah's, who always concluded his Opry act with, "I'm goin' back to the wagon, boys—these shoes are killin' me." Many and many a time in our country store back in Arkansas I heard a "good ole boy" stand up and stretch and repeat the Duke's line.

A middle-aged woman in too-tight stretch pants is admiring Elvis' "solid-gold" Cadillac. "It was worth comin' all the way down here to see that," she squeals.

Below the museum is the Country Music Association's Media Center, where serious researchers listen to vintage records and comb through manuscripts and clippings from bygone days. There you may find a correspondent from *Time* or *Fortune*, a graduate student toiling on a doctoral dissertation, a book writer pushing a deadline for a major publication.

Step across the room and look at the magazines and journals in the racks. You probably didn't know so many were covering the industry. The biggest is *Country Music Magazine* with 675,000 circulation. Doc Carter would have been impressed.

When you're done in the Media Center and through gawkin' at Elvis' solid-gold Cadillac in the museum, step outside in the sunlight and gaze across the street. You can see Barbara Mandrell's Number One Gift Shop in the World—it looks a block long. And you'll see Conway Twitty's Record Shop with a speaker booming an old prison ballad by Conway.

"She killed a man an for the baby's sake I took the blame." In either store you can buy novelty car tags announcing "Jesus Saves" or urging you to "Eat Mo' Possum."

Close by is the Wax Museum of Country-music luminaries. Up the block is a citified barnyard where anyone can sing or play before a sidewalk crowd and pass the hat as the old-timers used to do.

Blasting from a nearby boot is a barker from a tour company: "Come along, folks, and see the homes of the stars. Webb Pierce, Minnie Pearl, Hank Williams Jr., Hank Snow, the Reverend Jimmie Snow . . . See them all the many more. Hurry, hurry, the air-conditioned bus leaves in five minutes. Get your tickets here . . . Hurry . . . Hurry."

You also can get tour buses for Printer's Alley— Nashville's Bourbon Street—Tootsie's Orchid Lounge, where many stars hung out in the old days, and the Ryman Auditorium, where the Opry played before it moved to the new Opry House on the grounds of Opryland USA.

Opryland USA

Across town off Briley Parkway you can eye the memorabilia of Hank Snow, Mary Robbins, and Patsy Cline in the Opryland Museum. Then step over to Roy Acuff's place and take a gander at the "King's" old guitars, fiddles, show bills, and much more. There in a display case is the Acuff family Bible opened to the "Bird" verse, Jeremiah 12:9. Roy lives alone in an adjoining apartment. If you hang around long enough, he might stroll by.

For Country-music buffs Opryland is 241 acres of paradise. You'll love the bright, bouncy, bubbly music presented by 400 young singers and musicians performing in theaters scattered around the grounds. Broadway could "benefit" from

"Opryland's upbeat atmosphere", says the *Wall Street Journal*.

On this steamy day in August a husband-and-wife team are singing and cracking cornies at Martin's Outdoor Theater. The crowd on the split-log benches roars at hearing, "Hit's so hot today I saw an ole bird pulli' a worm out of the ground with a potholder." And "Hit's so dry that I seed two trees fightin' over a dog".

Listen to an imitation of Johnny Cash: "A lot of folks asked me why I wrote that song *Ring of Fire*. It was a mistake. I got my Ben Gay mixed up with Preparation H." Actually Merle Kilgore wrote the song, but nobody is checking history today.

Move over to Country Music USA, a toe-tapping, hand-trip down memory lane. The young performers dress and sing like the greats they portray. A staid "Carter Family" harmonizes on *Will the Circle Be Unbroken?* A young "Hank Williams" in white hat bemoans *Your Cheatin' Heart*. A bird-like Skeeter Davis warbles *It Wasn't God Who Made Honky-Tonk Angels*, and much, much more.

The big brick-walled Opry House graces the eastern side of Opryland with the largest television studio in the world. Pew-type curving benches will seat 4,400 people. The 110-foot stage holds 50 microphones connected to a mammoth console. Backstage the stars have dressing rooms, a lounge, and their own post office.

Seven Opry shows run each weekend during most of the year, with Saturday-night performances the year around. Almost a million people drive an average of a thousand miles round-trip to see a live Opry performance. The Opry is the oldest, longest-running, and most successful year-around, single music show in America.

Country Music's Most Prestigious "Club"

For country entertainers Opry membership is the top of the heap. Each artist appears about 26 weekends each year—some more, some less. Beloved Minnie Pearl once did shows in San Francisco, Denver, and Kansas City and then on Saturday night arrive cavorting across the stage wearing her $1.98 hat and hollering, "Howdee. I'm jist so glad to be hyar."

No costume designer or dress censor hovers backstage to check performers before they go on. Roy Acuff cottons to a tie, dapper sport coat, and boots. Hank Snow wouldn't be caught dead without his rhinestones. Stonewall Jackson, under his dark, wide-brimmed leather hat, looks as though he is a cowboy arriving in Dodge City on a Saturday night in 1880. Grandpa Jones would be lost without his floppy hat and suspendered jeans: "Everything I have on is new—well, all but these britches. They've stuck to me through thick and thin. I'm not gonna let 'em down now."

Dolly Parton, who has her own Dollywood in eastern Tennessee, is a fluff of cotton candy or a voluptuous Daisy Mae in a close-fitting jumpsuit. Connie Smith is the epitome of modesty in a long gown. Stu Phillips in a three-piece suit looks right out of the executive suite. Opry stars are a special cast of characters with images and dress suited to personal taste, musical styles, and how they think the fans want to see them.

The Opry is a sort of organized confusion: One group performs while other musicians wander around in the wings talking, shaking hands, slapping each other on the back, and sometimes tickling the announcer while he's giving a commercial or announcing a station break. Behind the performers sit friends and relatives, visiting press, presidents of fan clubs, and other celebrities stopping by to catch a few acts.

Nothing in show business can possibly match the Opry. "If you sat down to design a successful show, you would probably do just the opposite of the way we do it," says General Manager Hal Durham. Why? Because the Opry attempts to recreate, albeit on an exaggerated scale, the bygone good times when neighbors gathered in somebody's home or at the crossroads country store to enjoy a Saturday night of music and good friends.

The Opry, however, is more than this. The fiddling guitar-picking, the comedy, the clogging, the old-time ballads, and the hymns do help create a nostalgic atmosphere of earlier times. But the electronically amplified instruments, the drums, and the sexually suggestive lyrics of some singers displease many traditionalists, who complain that Country music has become too slick, sleazy, and commercial. Some fans also cringe when a performer does a honky-tonk cheating song and then turns saint for *Amazing Grace*. On balance, however, a lot of people seem to like the Opry the way it runs, for the fans keep arriving.

The Opry Goes on the Air

Since its founding the Opry has been broadcast by clear channel WSM Radio, which first went on the air at 7 p.m. Monday, October 5, 1925. WSM hired announcer George D. Hay away from WLS Chicago, where he had started the WLS "National Barn Dance." Hay, a former Memphis newspaper-man, was given free reign to develop programming.

One afternoon, so the story goes, an old, white-bearded man, carrying a black case, dropped by. It was Uncle Jimmy Thompson, 80 and blind in one eye. He said he could "fiddle the taters off a vine" and offered a demonstration.

"Well, let's hear it,' smiled Hay.

Uncle Jimmy opened the case, removed a pair of rattlesnake rattles and a piece of red flannel—"keeps ole Betsy warm at night", he said. He took out his fiddle and bow and struck up a tune. When he finished, Hay asked whether he knew any more.

"Shucks, I've got a thousand," the old man replied. Hay invited him back the next evening to play before the microphone.

On November 28, 1925, Uncle Jimmy led off with a rousing hoedown. After an hour Hay wondered whether he wasn't getting tired. "Shucks, no," the old man said. "A man don't get warmed up in an hour. I won an eight-day fiddling contest down at Dallas and here's my blue ribbon to prove it." Within week WSM had received letters and telegrams from every state in the nation.

Billing himself the "Solemn Ole Judge" though he was only 30, Hay began building an old-time Country cast. He signed Dr. Humphrey Bates, a country physician, and his group as the first band to play on WSM. He found banjo-playing "Uncle" Dave Macon driving a freight wagon. Uncle Dave, who knew as many songs as Uncle Jimmy did, was adept at naming performers. He termed himself "The Dixie Dewdrop". Uncle Jimmy remained, well, "Uncle Jimmy." Dr. Bates and his band became the "Gully Jumpers"; another group the "Dixie Clodhoppers"; a duo of brothers, "Sam and Kirk McGee from Sunny Tennessee." Sam McGee tells how they were discovered. "They came down to our farm and said they wanted players outstanding in the field. That's where they found us—out standing in the field."

"Judge" Hay's old-time music didn't please some of Nashville's city fathers, who complained that the players were projecting a bad image of Nashville and asked WSM to take them off the air. Hay asked listeners whether they wanted the fiddlers, pickers, and singers to continue. Letters and telegrams of support poured in. WSM's management said the program would remain.

By the fall of 1927 Hay was paying 25 musicians five dollars each to perform on WSM's "Saturday-Night Barn Dance." Immediately before the show, WSM broadcast "The Music Appreciation Hour", a program of opera, symphonic, and light classical music. One evening Hay announced, "For the past hour we've been listening to music taken largely from Grand Opera. Now we will present the 'Grand Ole Opry.'" And the Grand Ole Opry it has been for more than 60 years.

The Solemn Ole Judge, Uncle Jimmy, Dr. Bates, and Uncle Dave Macon were familiar names in Depression-ridden America and during World War II. Listening to them and other Opry performers became a ritual for many of us who couldn't go anywhere else on Saturday night. One of their fans was a boy in Plains, GA. Years later President Jimmy Carter stood on the Opry stage and said, "My biggest dream as a boy was to stand where I'm standing tonight."

The Opry Founders Go "Off the Air"

With the passing years the oldtimers began dying off. The first to go was Uncle Jimmy in 1931. Known to be a heavy drinker, one night he passed out from imbibing strong drink and froze to death, according to one story. His family claimed he caught pneumonia when his house caught on fire and he had to run outside in his longjohns. Dr. Bates died in 1936, seconds after telling his son, "I'm leaving this world."

Uncle Dave Macon, who called himself a religious man, carried whiskey in his little black satchel "grip" right on stage. He and Deford Bailey, a black performer, often traveled and did shows together. If a hotel refused Deford a room, Uncle Dave's would say, "He's my valet. He stays with me, or I'm leaving." Deford usually remained.

Uncle Dave played at the Opry until three weeks before he died in 1952. Today a monument to the Dixie Dewdrop stands along a highway outside Nashville. With a bar of music at the top and a banjo underneath, it has a profile of the familiar face with his gold-toothed smile. The bottom caption is the title of one of Uncle Dave's favorite hymns, *How Beautiful Heaven Must Be.*

Judge Hay frequently had to remind Opry performers to "keep it down to earth, boys." In explaining his philosophy he said, "We try to keep it [the music] homey. Many of our geniuses come from the simple folk who adhere to the fundamental principles of . . . the Ten Commandments. The Grand Ole Opry expresses these qualities which come to us from these good people."

As the Opry became more famous under Judge Hay, fans began arriving in the corridors of WSM on Saturday night. National Life built a 500-seat observation studio so fans could watch the performance. When the audience outgrew that, the Opry moved to a theater, later to a tabernacle with a sawdust floor, and then to the War Memorial Auditorium, which seated 3,000. When this hall proved to be too small, the world's most popular Country in 1943 show took up weekend residence in the downtown Ryman Auditorium

For 40 years the Solemn Ole Judge presided over every Opry broadcast. Many listeners began knowing by heart Judge Hay's closing midnight recitation:

That's all for now, friends . . .
Because the tall pines pine
And the pawpaws pause

And the bumblebees bumble all around,
The grasshoppers hop
And the eavesddropper drop
While, gently, the ole cow slips away . . .

George D. Hay closed by saying "So long for now!" Hay died on Wednesday, May 8, 1968, at his home.in Virginia. Saturday night Opry announcer Grant Turner, who Hay had trained, delivered a tribute:

"He called himself the Solemn Ole Judge. If he was solemn, it was only in the face of those who sought to change or corrupt the purity of the barn dance ballads he sought to preserve. We, the performers and friends of the Grand Ole Opry, salute the memory of one whose influence is felt on the stage of the Opry tonight—the Solemn Ole Judge, George D. Hay."

The Preacher and the Gambler

One night on the Opry, Uncle Dave Macon recalled a little history: "Now this tabernacle whar we play was built by Cap'n Tom Ryman for the preacher Sam Jones. Cap'n Tom had six steamboats on the Cumberland River. You ought to have see that wharf lined with horses and mules and wagons hauling freight to them boats and bringin' it back.

"Sam Jones preached the Bible so straight that Cap'n Tom went and poured all his whiskey in the river. And he took them card tables and burned 'em up—clean up. All from hearin' Sam Jones preach and gittin' converted." That was how this song came to be written by Cap'n Tom's deckhands:

Cap'n Tom Ryman was a steamboat man,
But Sam Jones sent him to the heavenly land,
Oh, sail away . . .

Uncle Dave gave only the bare bones of one of the most thrilling dramas in the history of American revivalism. San Jones was the greatest evangelist the South produced before Billy Graham. Tom Ryman was his prize convert. Jones said for years afterward, "If Tom gets to heaven before I do and the Lord asks me what I'm doing there, I'll just hunt Tom up, put him on my shoulders, and say, 'Lord, here's my apology for being here.'"

A converted alcoholic, Sam Jones arrived in Nashville in March 1885 and held a revival at the Tulip Street Methodist Church. The church filled rapidly. So many had to be turned away that local ministers and laypeople promised to set up a large tent if he would return. Some Nashville ministers, however, opposed the colorful revivalist. One prominent pastor said he enjoyed a circus but preferred not to attend one in which Jones was ringmaster. Another minister complained about Jones' use of "coarse wit and humor to spice his sermons."

The common people, however, loved the black-eyed, heavy-jawed preacher for the same reason that the society bunch despised him. "I believe in puttin' the fodder down low where the cows can get it," Jones often said.

Other memorable remarks included these:

"I like a fast horse, but may the Good Lord deliver me from a fast woman."

"You little, stingy, narrow-hided rascals. A fly could sit on the bridge of your nose and paw you in one eye and kick you in the other. You could look through a keyhole with both eyes and not be cross-eyed either."

"If some of those old moneymongers get to heaven, they'll be out before breakfast, diggin up the golden streets."

The Hermitage Club, where liquor was served and members gambled, was the most prestigious club in the city. The most notorious slumlords and liquor dealers in the city belonged to the club. Jones went after the Hermitage elite, tooth and nail:

"If I had a church member who was a member of the Hermitage Club, I would have him out of the club or out of the church. Show me a pious man that belongs to it and I will eat the whole business, bricks and all. I believe religion is incompatible with those things."

Jones proved that 68 of 81 liquor dealers in Nashville were members of churches and listed the guilty ones by denomination. Many who arrived to hear Jones out of hatred stayed to be converted. His May 1885 meetings averaged almost 10,000 attendees a day—one sixth of the city's population. In almost every service 250 or more walked the sawdust aisles and knelt before the rough altar.

Every one of Tom Ryman's boats had a bar and gambling tables in which prominent Nashvillians could indulge their pleasures apart from family and disapproving ministers. Ryman, also a charitable man, gave large sums to churches. He was counted a pillar in the business community and a leader in Nashville society.

Upset by reports of Jones' preaching Ryman took a gang of ruffians to the revival tent to break up the meeting. That evening Jones preached on a mother's love and hit Ryman in a soft spot. The captain was one of the first to the altar as he cried for forgiveness.

Tom Ryman never did anything halfway. Closing his saloon and bars, he had gallons of expensive whiskey, cardtables, and gambling devices dumped into the river. He turned his riverbank saloon into a place for Christian meetings and temperance rallies. He opened a chapel for prayer meetings on every boat and christened one steamer, "The Sam Jones."

Ryman then started raising money to build a tabernacle for

future meetings Jones held. The Union Gospel Tabernacle was opened in 1890 at a cost of around $100,000, with much of the cash stemming from Ryman. The first night about 5,000 arrived at the building, with an overflow crowd standing outside and straining to hear.

The greatest revival occurred in 1898. On opening night the tabernacle again was jammed. Within a week 15,000 were trying to get in. Hundreds were converted. Thousands of men vowed to abstain from liquor and gambling. To signify their resolve they marched in a street parade led by Jones and Ryman.

Besides Sam Jones the most famous American ministers of that day preached in the tabernacle. When Tom Ryman died in 1905, Sam Jones held his funeral there and proposed that the tabernacle be named "Ryman Auditorium." Jones died a year later.

Revivalism waned in America. Under trustee ownership the Ryman became the cultural center of Nashville. The great opera companies of the world performed there, as did the most famous symphonies and theater casts.

The "Mother Church" of Country Music

By 1940 Nashville had the other auditoriums and cultural tastes were changing. The famous Ryman was empty most weekends until the Grand Ole Opry moved there in 1943. The next 31 years would see the greatest Country musicians and comedians perform on the historic stage. Red Foley, Bill Monroe, Ernest Tubb, Cowboy Copas, Minnie Pearl, Roy Acuff, Hank Williams, Patsy Cline, Hank Snow, Tex Ritter, Connie Smith, Loretta Lynn, Billy Walker, Dolly Parton, the Wilburn Brothers, the Willis Brothers, and Skeeter Davis were among those who made the Ryman the "Mother Church of

Country Music."

For 50 years no sermon had been delivered from the Ryman stage. Then in the fall of 1972 Reverend Jimmy Snow talked with Opry officials about taping a weekly radio program to follow the Opry. Once known for wild living, Hank Snow's son had become the most popular minister in the Country-music community.

The Opry now was on two nights a week. Opry manager Bud Wendell invited Snow to do his program after the Friday-night Opry.

Two weeks later, at 11:05 p.m., the Opry announcer closed the last regular segment and said, "Good evening, ladies and gentlemen, welcome to the first broadcast of 'Grand Ole Gospel Time', coming to you live from the stage of the Grand Ole Opry House in Nashville, TN. Here is your host, Pastor Jimmie Snow."

Jimmie quickly introduced Johnny Cash who sang, *Take Your World and Turn It Around,* while the audience clapped. After his church choir sang, Jimmie delivered a short sermon.

Every Friday night after that an Opry member sang and gave a personal testimony of faith. Then Jimmie preached a short sermon and invited people to repent and accept Christ as their Savior.

The Ryman was a hot box in summer and an ice box in winter. It could not hold all the people who wanted to see and hear the Opry.

A decision was made to relocate to a new and larger building near Briley Parkway.

The move was accepted as necessary, but disposing of the Ryman caused a controversy. Some proposed that it be torn down and the bricks be used for building near the new Opry House. Roy Acuff said he would attend church there every Sunday. The idea to preserve the Ryman as a museum was finally accepted as the most practical. Also for sentimental reasons a chunk of the old oak stage from where Sam Jones had preached and entertainment greats had performed would be transplanted to the stage of the new Opry House.

The Opry Says "Goodbye"

The last Opry in the Ryman was set for Friday, March 15, 1974. The premier performance in the new Opry House would be the following evening with President Richard Nixon as an honored guest.

The final evening in the old Ryman truly was a memorable occasion. Such tears hadn't been shed there since Tom Ryman's funeral. The show dragged on until almost midnight, when the last song of the Opry was sung and Jimmie Snow's "Grand Ole Gospel Time" went on stage.

Hank Snow, Johnny Cash, and his daughter, Rosanne and three generations of Carters joined Jimmie and the church choir for the special service. After they all sang, *Will the Circle Be Unbroken?* each entertainer said a few words. Bowing to the preachers of the past Johnny Cash gave a patriotic recitation of *That Ragged Old Flag.*

When Jimmie Snow began preaching, the time was almost 1 a.m. The building and the aisles were still packed. "It's been a long time since Sam Jones stood here and preached hell fire and brimstone to sinners," he said, "and a long time since Captain Tom Ryman was converted and inspired to build this old tabernacle." Preaching from 2 Corinthians 5:17 Jimmie compared the moving of the Opry to the life-changing experience of becoming a Christian.

The choir began singing a song of invitation, *Just As I Am.* Jimmie invited those who wanted to receive salvation to stand. So many stood that for him or Johnny Cash to count them all was impossible. Instead of an altar call Jimmie asked penitents to say a sinner's prayer:

Jesus, I am a sinner and cannot save myself. I stand on your promise that you will come into my heart. I give myself to you. I love you, Jesus.

Then as the choir hummed softly, Jimmie told the tired and tearful audience, "I pray that you will be so touched with the hand of God that you'll never forget tonight so long as you life. The last words as we leave this blessed old building should be: 'And all the people said, Amen.'"

The fervent "Amens" reverberated all around the old hall. The crowd moved out slowly and solemnly with many still crying.

An era had ended. A new one had begun for the Opry and its myriad of fans.

A New Era Begins

From the old Ryman was where I and so many others heard the Grand Ole Opry in the 1930s and 1940s. When I went to Nashville more than 40 years later, the building was easy to find. I paid the $1 entry fee and slipped into the stream of reverent visitors. Walking softly down the aisle I stood on the historic stage for a few moments. I stood just in front of the painting of the old red barn with the big logo, WSM GRAND OLE OPRY. I closed my eyes and heard the Solemn Ole Judge welcoming the radio audience to "the Grand Ole Opry, comin' to you live from Nashville, Tennessee." I heard Minnie Pearl cry, "Howdee" and Roy Acuff give the lonesome whistle of *The Wabash Cannonball.*

My memory raced back to Big Creek Valley, where I gathered with family and neighbors around the big console radio at the Kents. I heard Grampa Tom stamping his feet and hollering to the Gully Jumpers, "Play it, boys!"

The spell broke. I followed a line of people backstage to see the long mural painting termed, "Saturday Night in Hillbilly Heaven." Walking slowly down the runway I gazed at the departed greats of County music. There was Judge George D. Hay, Hank Williams, Maybelle Carter, Red Foley, Patsy Cline, and more.

Awe-stricken fans around me spoke in reverent whispers: "There's Patsy. Isn't she beautiful?" And, "Is that Maybelle Carter? I've heard of her all my life, but I've never seen her picture."

I stood aside and listened and watched as the lines of fans shuffled by. They, like me, were remembering and fantasizing the "good ole" days when the Grand Ole Opry brightened our long-ago Saturday nights back in the country places of our childhoods.

Chapter 4
Getting Right with God

On a cold and foggy February night in 1937, a boy was born in a Salvation Army Hospital in Halifax, Nova Scotia. The boy's father, Clarence E. "Hank" Snow, peddled fish and gave guitar lessons to support his family. He couldn't afford even a baby bed when mother Minnie and the baby returned home. Little Jimmie slept in a bureau drawer.

Father-and-Son Act

When the boy was 2, Hank plopped him on a stack of Coca-Cola cases at a music show and announced, "Ladies and gentlemen, may I present my son, Jimmie Rodgers Snow, named after my idol in Country music." With Hank accompanying on the guitar, little Jimmie belted out *Jesus Loves Me*, a song he had learned at the Anglican church on a hill overlooking Halifax Harbor.

Billing himself "The Singing Ranger", Hank was one of a dozen rising young Country stars—including Gene Autry, Bob Willis, Eddie Arnold, Red Foley, Hank Williams, and T. Tex Tyler—who were building their style around the lonesome railroad songs of little Jimmie's namesake, the tubercular brakeman from Meridian, MS. Being so far away, in remote eastern Canada, Hank was far removed from the centers of Country music. But he was determined. By Jimmie's first birthday Hank had a recording contract with Victor and was making show tours across the eastern provinces.

The Snows now were on the road. Hank and Jimmie performed. Mother Minnie dealt with the bookings and box office and then went ahead to rent a theater or hall in the next town. She was there selling tickets and programs when father and son arrived.

Hank and Jimmie swept on stage in matching cowboy outfits—broad-brimmed white hats, yellow kerchiefs, tailored white suits, and boots with a mirror finish. Jimmie opened the show with "Good evening, ladies and gentlemen". Then Hank took over, with his son returning later for duets.

Hank was a perfectionist. Jimmie had to know his lines word-perfect. His enunciation and rhythm had to be flawless and his costume spotless. Once an older boy lured Jimmie to a creek and pushed him in just before the show. When Hank saw his son's wet and muddy costume, he made him parade before the crowd in a dress and then whipped him soundly.

They went to West Virginia for a few months and sang on WWVA, Wheeling. Then Hank took their savings and bought a trick horse, a tent, a portable grandstand, a truck, and a semi. With a hired band and a juggler, they hit the Canadian circuit again.

Hank did rope tricks and daredevil riding acts. At his father's cue Jimmie would jump on the stirrup to spin a rope and sing a duet with his dad. Jimmie also assisted the juggler with a dangerous knife trick.

After a couple of years Hank left Minnie and Jimmie at home and sought fortune in Hollywood. The publicity men took everything he had. He moved on to KRLD Dallas' Big-D Jamboree. In 1948 when Jimmie was 11, Hank sent for his wife and son to travel to Texas.

For several months the family slept with their horse, Shawnee, in the truck which Hank kept parked in front of a nightspot where he also entertained. Jimmie sang with Hank in the Roundup Club and at the Silver Spur down the street. The latter was operated by Jack Ruby, who later shot Lee Harvey Oswald before television cameras.

When not assisting his father Jimmie sat at tables with drinking patrons or danced with women customers. During the day he played hookey from school and robbed newspaper boxes downtown.

Good Samaritan Ernest Tubb

At KRLD Hank became good buddies with Ernest Tubb, the "Texas Troubadour." Ernest had a son, Justin, a year older than Jimmie. Ernest and hank also shared a common admiration for the late Jimmie Rodgers. The brakeman's Widow had helped Ernest get a recording contract and even had lent him one of Jimmie Rodgers' guitars. When the Snows arrived, Ernest was making money from *I'm Walking the Floor Over You, I'll Get Along Somehow* and *Take Me Back and Try Me One More Time.*

Ernest had made a profession of faith and been baptized in a Baptist church at 14. But like so many other Country singers, he had let music take the place of church. Nevertheless, he would help anybody and sometimes gave away more money than he made. Fellow entertainer Cal Smith said, "Ernest doesn't go to church anymore. But if he doesn't go to heaven, there isn't a heaven."

Ernest joined the Grand Ole Opry and paid the travel expenses for the Snows to go to Nashville. Hank went on the WSM stage in 1950 and rocketed to fame with a railroad song that was pure vintage Jimmie Rodgers. *I'm Movin On* topped the charts for 29 straight weeks.

Hank Snow's Son:
Voted "Most Unlikely to Succeed"

Hank and Minnie Snow bought a house in Madison, a northern suburb of Nashville. Jimmie brought to Tennessee all the bad habits he had learned in Texas. Now a sixth-grader, he took cards and dice to school and ran his own "casino" in the schoolyard during recess. Inside, when he was supposed to be studying, he picked wallets from pockets and purses. At test time he gave some victims part of their money back for the privilege of copying their papers. Hank and Minnie didn't know their son had become an accomplished gambler, con man, and thief.

Jimmie found an easy way to slip cash from his father's billfold at night. With the money the boy bought a gun and hired a taxi to ride around Nashville after school. Jimmie carried the gun in his book bag and sometimes let his classmates have a peek. Bringing a gun to school was unheard of in those days.

Sometimes he'd cash a $100 bill at the lunch counter and wave the currency around to get attention. When he was asked where he got the money, he'd toss his shoulders and grin, "Don't you know that my daddy is Hank Snow?" In the eighth grade they voted Jimmie "Most Unlikely to Succeed." School authorities also caught on and booted him from one school to another.

For Jimmie Rodgers Snow, in the early 1950s, the center of everything was the Opry. It was the one place he believed he belonged—the place where he met his extended "family."

Standing in the stage wings, he heard Bill Monroe and the

Bluegrass Boys, Roy Acuff and the Smoky Mountain Boys, and a host of other "uncle" and "aunt" figures. He howled at comedians Jamup and Honey and at Minnie Pearl swirling her skirt and telling stories about "Brother" in Grinder's Switch. He tapped his foot to Red Foley's singing *Peace in the Valley* and hummed behind Hank Williams' *Cold, Cold Heart.* Between acts he ran around backstage with other Opry kids.

At the Opry a big moment occurred for Hank Snow. "Ladies and gentlemen, I'm proud to present my son, Jimmie Rodgers Snow." Jimmie still was a little young, but he sang well. Everybody expected that he would be asked to join the Opry in a few years.

But Jimmie now was more interested in a neighborhood girl. Her protective parents would only permit him to take her to their Assembly of God church.

The hymns didn't affect him. He had heard entertainers sing the same songs and then head out with a woman and a bottle. But the preaching made him miserable, for a voice kept nagging, *Boy, you can't fool God. He knows all about you.*

Jimmie attended the church for a while and then drifted away after he broke up with the girl. At 17 he started boozing and never thought he would become an alcoholic like Red Foley and Hank Williams. The liquor made him feel good and snapped inhibitions.

Jimmie knew about the drinking and the drug problems of Hank Williams and Red Foley. All the Opry families did.

The Sad Saga of Hank Williams

Hank Williams seemed to be in the worst shape. On road trips, fellow entertainers would remove bottles hidden in his bags, refuse to let him order drinks in restaurants, and escort him to the hotel, where they locked him in his room until time for the show. He outsmarted his protectors for a while by concealing whiskey in shaving lotion and cologne bottles. When they caught on, he found other ways to get liquor. Hank's buddies were afraid he wouldn't last long, but his fans thought he would go on forever.

Hank Williams now was the biggest voice in Country music. *Cold, Cold Heart, Hey, Good Lookin', Your Cheatin' Heart,* and other records were making him a millionaire. Yet his life was spinning out of control—a replay of Jimmie Rodgers' last days—thanks to whiskey, drugs, and easy women. On top of this, in January 1952 he had to have back surgery. Then he fell and re-injured his back. When infection spread through his body, doctors, knowing his weakness for wild living, gave him only a year to live.

Wife Audrey filed for divorce from Hank. In May the decree was issued. It gave her a whopping settlement and custody of their 3-year-old son, Hank Jr. In December the Opry fired him for drunkenness and irresponsibility just before his *Jambalaya* was declared the top-selling record of the year.

Hank Williams must have known he was going. Riding in car with several other performers, who were trying to keep him sober for a performance, he suddenly began singing his trademark hymn *I Saw the Light.* Then he paused and with sad eyes looked over and said, "Minnie [Pearl], there ain't no more light for me."

At the time Hank was engaged to marry his second wife, Billie Jean Jones Eshlimar. He also was having an affair with a Nashville woman named Bobbie Jett, who became pregnant. Hank reportedly signed a custody agreement for the child three days before he married Billie Jean.

Hank hired a man to drive him in a Cadillac to a January 1, 1953, show date in Canton, Ohio. They stopped to get gas and a shot of painkiller for his back. After Hank became quiet, the driver checked to see whether he was all right and found him dead in the back seat. The autopsy linked his heart failure at 29 to excessive drinking.

That New Year's night in Canton a spotlight played on an empty stage while the dead singer's voice emerged on the loudspeakers singing, *I Saw the Light*. Many in the audience sobbed.

Hank's Country-music pals told about how Hank could move from a honky-tonk song to a spiritual—singing like a devil one minute and a saint the next. While he didn't care for formal religion, he could get emotional talking about God. Some said he must have been a believer, for how else could he have written *I Saw the Light* and *Mansion Over the Hilltop*?

On a cold winter day, 25,000 fans sought the 2,750 seats for Hank Williams' funeral in Montgomery, AL's municipal auditorium. Ernest Tubb sang *Beyond the Sunset;* Roy Acuff did *I Saw the Light*; and a quavering Red Foley poured out *Peace in the Valley*. Four women fainted and a fifth fell at the foot of the casket and had to be carried from the auditorium in hysteria.

Two days after Hank's funeral, Billie Jean's baby, Cathy, was born and adopted by Hank's mother, Lilly Stone. When Lilly died two years later, Hank's sister, Irene, handed little Cathy over the state. She was placed with a foster family. Later she was adopted by a couple from Mobile, AL. Not until she became 21 and received a $2,000 inheritance from the Lily Stone estate did she have any clue to her famous parentage. In 1980 she discovered she was the daughter of the famous Hank Williams.

In death Hank Williams founded a cult. His divorced wife and his widow made special personal appearances. MGM produced a movie, *Your Cheatin' Heart*, which made no mention of booze, drugs, womanizing, and divorce. His records sold faster than ever. Ironically, the biggest seller the year after his death was *I'll Never Get Out of This World Alive.*

Hank Williams died at age 29, just 13 years older than Jimmie Snow, yet Jimmie saw no similarity between Hank's dissolute lifestyle and his own. Jimmie went right on drinking.

Hank Snow Disinherits His Son

Hank Snow still hadn't realized what a wild life his son was leading. He encouraged Jimmie to sign up with promoter Colonel Tom Parker, who had in his stable Mother Maybelle and the Carter Sisters, Marty Robbins, a new Country comic named Andy Griffith, and other talent. In Memphis Colonel Parker picked up Elvis Presley, the young hip-wiggler from Mississippi. Elvis had appeared on the Opry and hoped to be invited into membership. After he wiggled his hips on stage, an Opry official advised him to get a job as a truck driver, but the response of the audience to Elvis' stage gyrations gave Parker other ideas.

The Colonel booked Elvis and Jimmie Snow together. They made a strange pair. Jimmie smoked, drank, and cursed, while Elvis abstained. Elvis knew church songs and quoted the Bible like he was a preacher. Both liked girls.

Elvis ran Country, pop, and rhythm-and-blues music together with a fast beat and set the rock-and-roll style that made him famous. Backed by a frenzied drum beat, the sensual crooning, howling, wailing, hip-wiggling Elvis drove some teen-aged girls and women into hysteria.

In Jacksonville, FL, a pack of screaming women chased Jimmie and Elvis across a football field. The two entertainers literally had to run for their lives.

The crafty Colonel had signed an unusual management contract with Elvis and gave him one-half of the singer's receipts. When the Colonel saw what he had, he dropped Jimmie and the others and took Elvis on full time.

Having nothing better to do, Jimmie went with his father and Ernest Tubb to the annual memorial celebration Hank and Ernest had started in Meridian, MS, to honor the memory of Jimmie Rodgers. After a few drinks, Jimmie Snow told one of Hank Thompson's band members, "I can't sing." The picker slipped him a couple of Benzedrines for a "lift." Jimmie asked for another and another. By year's end he was hooked.

Hank began getting phone calls from bars to which Jimmie owned money. A police officer arrived at the house on a complaint that Jimmie and some friends had gotten drunk and nailed all the furniture in a motel room to the ceiling.

Hank laid down one ultimatum after another, but Jimmie ignored them all. One night Hank followed Jimmie downtown and watched him go into a club. Hank slipped into a phone booth and warned the manager. "Get that underage boy out in two minutes, or I'm calling the police."

"Son, I've taken you out of my will," Hank finally informed his only child. As Jimmie sat stunned, Hank assured him that he would always have a place to eat and sleep. "My stepfather threw me out of my home," he recalled. "I'll never do that to you."

On the evening of January 3, 1956, Jimmie headed for a drive-in movie. Slowing to turn left across four-lane Dickinson Road near the theater, he was hit headon by a drunk driver fleeing police at 105 miles an hour. The nub on the steering wheel shattered against Jimmie's chest. The steering column was driven into his thigh and pushed the bone out on the other side. He spent 38 days in the hospital, got more than 10,000 get-well letters from fans, and unchanged, went home on crutches.

A Prayer of Desperation

Jimmie fell back on the pills and booze. Then at the fall deejay convention held every year in Nashville, he ran into some old friends from WWVA, Wheeling, WV. Wilma Lee and Stoney Cooper had arrived in Nashville to join the Opry. They brought along their beautiful, long-haired, 15-year-old daughter, Carol. Jimmie fell for the girl.

On learning that the Coopers were to accompany his father on a show tour across Canada, Jimmie took a new interest in music. Because they were the only teen-agers in the group, he and Carol spent a lot of time together.

For reasons he couldn't understand, his show-business career began picking up after his return from Canada. RCA offered a recording contract. An invitation arrived to sing on the Opry. Would membership be next? Tennessee Gov. Frank Clement recommended him to famed drama teacher, Elia Kazan. Lawrence Welk asked him to Hollywood for a television appearance. Jimmie returned home, shared his excitement with Carol Cooper, and then went out and got drunk.

A week later the Coopers let him take Carol to see *The Ten Commandments*. He was so taken with the biblical story that he saw the movie 10 times. He started reading the Bible every day. He took Carol to church. She was converted.

Later one evening he sat in his bedroom with his Bible open. "I wanted to throw myself on God's mercy," he recalls, "yet I was afraid. Afraid that if I did get saved, really saved, I would have to preach. How could a booze-hound, pill-head, and shirt-chaser like me become a preacher? It seemed impossible."

He talked to Carol about being a preacher's wife. She was agreeable.

On Wednesday night, November 27, 1957, Jimmie arrived

home drunk again. He wobbled into his room. "At 21 I had everything the world says should make you happy," he later wrote. "Youth, money, a famous name, friends like Elvis Presley, Tommy Sands, Bill Haley. A beautiful girl who said she would marry me. Opportunities opening to make it big on my own. Yet I had nothing and hated my wretched, miserable, empty self. Booze and pills had totally enslaved me. Dad had given up and disinherited me.

"Being cut off from Daddy's money didn't hurt me as much as did the realization that I had shattered all his dreams for me. He had waited so long to present his son as the newest member of the Grand Ole Opry. Now I was Jimmie Rodgers Snow—the Bum."

Jimmie reached into his pants pocket and pulled out the snub-nosed Smith-and-Wesson revolver he had carried for years. He stuck the gun barrel in his mouth and got set to pull the trigger but couldn't do it.

Throwing the gun on the bed, he lurched toward the door and staggered into the cool night air. Reaching the mailbox, he fell on his face and cried, "Help me, God! If You're real, help me, God!" He prayed louder and louder. Neighbors began turning on lights.

"I must have prayed an hour in the freezing cold. I would have stayed there all night, I was so desperate. But at some time, somehow, I reached out in faith to God. My mind cleared and I was filled with an overflowing peace. I knew my past had been forgiven and that my future belonged to Him. Not only had God accepted me, He also was going to use me in His service. Like Moses, I was going to be His spokesman."

He ran into the house and shouted, "Mother, I've found God! I'm going to be a preacher!"

Jarred awake, Minnie Snow looked at her prodigal and sighed, "Jimmie, you're going to have a nervous breakdown."

Jimmie drove to the house of Jay Alford, the pastor of the local Assembly of God church, and woke him up. "God has saved me, Brother Alford," he announced. "He wants me to be a preacher."

The pastor wanted him to attend the Assemblies of God Bible College in Springfield, MO. But Jimmie had not finished high school and wanted to get married first. When he and Carol realized her parents were not going to consent, they eloped. Angry and hurt, Stoney and Wilma Lee talked of having the marriage annulled. Hank and Minnie also were upset but said the newlyweds could live with them until they found a place. At the Opry Hank introduced them as husband and wife.

Jimmie's Preaching Debut

Jimmie's pastor invited him to preach at the church. Jimmie rehearsed his sermon, "Twelve Men and a Light", for his father. "Sounds good," Hank said, but he didn't attend the service.

The young couple moved into a trailer. Jimmie bargained with God. "Lord, if you want me to preach, get me invited somewhere by the first of September."

Near the end of August a woman from the church called and asked, "Would you and Carol come and sing next Friday night at the mission I've started downtown in a trailer park? And Jimmie, would you give your testimony?" Jimmie said *yes* and wrote down the address: Second Avenue near the Ryman Auditorium where the Opry was performing.

That night Jimmie stood up to face an audience of 22 who were sitting in folding chairs. To his right he could see people lining up for the Opry where his father and Carol's parents soon would go on stage. He kept one eye on the sidewalk and hoped none of the Opry entertainers would stop to listen. He still was afraid to give up show business since he knew he could make a living from it.

In October a revival preacher named Glen Miller attended the church. One night Miller interrupted his sermon and announced, "Jimmie and Carol Snow, I have a word from the Lord for you. You are to step out on faith and trust Him to provide."

Jimmie canceled his show dates and bought a big reference Bible. The following Thursday night he substituted for his pastor in a revival in a little church on Trinity Lane. His mother and Maybelle Carter were there to hear his sermon. It was over in four minutes.

As news spread that Hank Snow's son had become a minister, preaching invitations began arriving. Ezra Carter, Maybelle's husband, invited Jimmie to use his large library of Bible studies. Jimmie spent hours there as he asked Ezra questions and looked up interpretations of difficult verses. He also took correspondence courses from the Moody Bible Institute.

Jimmie Becomes an Evangelist

Jimmie never went to Bible college. For the next six years he and Carol crisscrossed the country and held revivals in Assemblies of God churches. Under their ministry thousands walked the sawdust trail.

Jimmie and Carol's first child, Vanessa, was born while Jimmie was away in a revival in St. Louis. Three weeks later mother and daughter joined him on the evangelistic circuit. They put the baby in a bassinet on the platform and held services.

At this time in the mid '60s, the Christian witness was weak among Country entertainers. Even those who wanted to be loyal to their church couldn't attend services regularly.

They were performing in some distant city at least every other Saturday night and could hardly get back to Nashville in time. At home Saturday-night performances on the Opry kept them up late. Because almost all were from out of town, few had local church connections. For their part most churches seemed neither to know nor care about reaching the Country entertainers and songwriters.

More than any other preacher in Nashville, Jimmie Snow understood the lifestyles of Country-music people. He knew them as members of the Opry "family" with their marital infidelities, divorces, boozing, and drug use. He believed many wanted to know God if only they could find someone who could point the way to the "Light" about which Hank Williams had sung so eloquently.

The Transformation of T. Texas Tyler

Jimmie and Carol were home between revivals when the phone jangled them awake early one morning. A deep growl slammed into Jimmie's ear: "Praise the Lord!" He remembered that sandpaper voice but couldn't place the name.

"Praise the Lord! Son, don't you know your old pal, Tex Tyler?"

T. Texas Tyler, of course, was Jimmie's roommate on a number of old show tours. A truly great Western artist who had sung in many Western movies, he was in a class with Gene Autry, Roy Rogers, Bob Willis, and Eddie Arnold. Billed as "the man with a million friends", Tex had scored with *Remember Me* in the '40s—which became his theme song— and had then hit in the early '50s with *A Deck of Cards*, which sent him to Carnegie Hall.

The last time Jimmie remembered being with Tex was for an afternoon matinee in El Paso. Afterward Tex had gone back to their room and run into the arms of waiting police. They booked him for smuggling drugs across the Mexican border and threw him into a padded cell. Tex didn't make the second performance.

"I just had to call and tell you I've been saved, son," Tex said over the phone. "You won't believe it, but I'm preaching just like you. Praise the Lord!"

Tex told of how after the arrest in El Paso he had gone from bad to worse. He was popping pills and boozing. Besides young Jimmie Snow, he had one other old friend who he knew was a genuine Christian. This was Carl "Deacon" Moore, a veteran deejay and music promoter. Deacon and Tex had frequently played golf together. Deacon usually managed to get in a word for the Lord. More than once he told Tex, "Buddy, think how much influence you could be in turning people to God if you should get saved." Tex always had brushed off Deacon's witness. Then he became desperate and called his friend.

"Deacon, I'm in trouble. I think I may kill myself. Can you come and see me?"

Tex lived in California's San Gabriel Valley. Deacon was south of Los Angeles at Huntington Beach. "I'm comin', Tex," he promised. "Hang on, 'til I get there."

Deacon found Tex drunk, running around the house, and screaming, "I'm going crazy! What am I gonna do?"

Deacon wasted no time. "Get down here on your knees. Repeat after me, 'God, I'm no good. I've tried everything else in the world and nothing has worked. It's either You, Lord, or nothin'. If You can change my life, now's the time."

Tex fell on his knees roaring drunk. He got up as sober as a preacher in a pulpit.

Tex lived only a few more years but proclaimed the gospel until the day he died.

Tex Tyler's call is what made Jimmie Snow believe God could do something among the Country musicians in Nashville. Perhaps God wanted him and Carol to start a church which would appeal to Country artists. It would be a place in which they could find the "peace in the valley" for which Red Foley still was searching.

Patsy Cline:
"I Need to Get Right with God"

Later that same year Jimmie and Carol were home again from the revival circuit. Down at the Opry Jimmie talked with Patsy Cline, then the biggest female star in the Country-music world. The year before, Billboard had named her the top female artist of the year. Talk was that she might succeed the reigning "Queen of Country Music", Kitty Wells.

One of Patsy's biggest hits was *I Fall to Pieces*. Now she was telling the Reverend Jimmie Snow, "I'm not happy. I need to get right with God."

"Well, the way is open, Patsy," he said. "Jesus died for you and wants to forgive you. Would you like to turn to Him now?"

"Not now," she demurred. "I'm not ready yet."

"I'll pray for you," Jimmie promised as Patsy hurried onto the stage for her next show.

Chapter 5
Peace in the Valley

Patsy Cline's real name was Virginia Patterson Hensley. A pretty, apple-cheeked girl with an open smile, she sprang from a poor family in Winchester, VA. Dropping out of high school to work to support her parents, she sang in churches, honky-tonks, and even on street corners.

In 1948, when Patsy was 16, she drove to Nashville with her sister and a family friend who wanted to get her an audition. They slept in the car and on park benches and ate peanut-butter sandwiches. Patsy sang for Roy Acuff, who let her perform on his radio program on WSM. The station management wanted her to stay over to audition as a possible regular on Roy's show, but she had to leave because they had barely enough money for gas to get home,

For the next five years Patsy sang with the Melody Playboys around Winchester. A stormy marriage to Gerald Cline lasted only three years. During that time Patsy's singing reputation grew. She appeared on the Ozark Jubilee, the Jimmy Dean Show, and several other regional television programs. Her song *Walkin' after Midnight* put her on the record charts. She married Charlie Dick, a Winchester man, and became pregnant. Now she simply wanted to settle down with Charlie and enjoy a quiet life.

Charlie didn't want to waste her talent. They moved to Nashville. She recorded *I Fall to Pieces*. With her warm, throbbing voice the song in 1960 became the number-one record.

Patsy Cline Tutors Loretta Lynn

Patsy was a soft touch for younger entertainers trying to make it in the business. One she befriended was Loretta Lynn, the coal-miner's daughter rom Kentucky. Loretta and her husband Mooney also had slept in their car and lived off sandwiches during their first trip to Nashville. Loretta's career caught fire. The Wilburn Brothers—Doyle and Teddy—put her on their syndicated TV show and got her a recording contract.

Some said Loretta was trying to be another Patsy Cline, but Patsy didn't seem to mind. Patsy taught her Kentucky friend how to walk on stage, how to play to a crowd, and how to walk off. Patsy often toted an extra blouse or skirt as she visited Loretta's house. "I was out shopping and bought one of these for myself. I just knew you'd like one, too," Patsy would say. The two became best friends.

In 1961 Patsy, then only 29 and the mother of two young children, was critically injured in a car accident. She was in the hospital almost six months. Loretta visited her and joked about Patsy's hit record, *I Fall to Pieces*. A week after leaving the hospital Patsy recorded another hit, *Crazy*.

Patsy Cline "Finds God"

Patsy apparently was going through another valley when she and Jimmie Snow talked backstage at the Opry. Jimmie had to leave for a revival but encouraged Patsy to attend the church which he and Carol attended. In early 1963 she went to the altar there and told friends that she had found God and was happy.

During another time at home, Jimmie talked with Lloyd "Cowboy" Copas, one of the best-liked Western singers on the Opry. Lean and lanky, Cowboy had joined the Opry in 1946 and made a hit with *My Filipino Baby.*

Jimmie knew Cowboy and his family well. Jimmy had run around with Cowboy's son, Gary, before Jimmie became a preacher. The young evangelist also was good friends with Randy Hughes, Cowboy's pilot son-in-law and the road manager for Patsy Cline and Billy Walker.

Hawkshaw Procrastinates

Harold "Hawkshaw" Hawkins, 43, was a old friend of the Snow family from West Virginia days; his wife, Jean, was a ranch girl from Oklahoma. Both were doing well in Country music. Jean arrived to hear Jimmie preach when he was holding a revival in Nashville. Hawkshaw always was "going to come" but never got around to it.

Hawkshaw sang in a deep-voiced Western style. His early recording of *Sunny Side of the Mountain* had become a Country classic. His distinctive stage garb was a black jacket with a hawk emblem on the back. The emblem symbolized his nickname.

When Jimmie visited, Cowboy and Jean were expecting their second child. In a talkative mood Hawkshaw said, "Jimmie, I'm going to tell you something nobody in Nashville knows. When I was a boy back in West Virginia, God called me to be an evangelist like you are. But I loved the music business so much that I ran out of that church and never returned."

"How's your life been since?" Jimmie asked.

"I've gone higher than I ever dreamed. But I've always known something important was missing."

"You know what it is," Jimmie reminded.

"Yes, I've left the Lord out of my life."

"Why don't you turn your life over to Him? He'll show you what's really best."

"I intend to do that," Hawkshaw declared. "Cowboy, Patsy Cline, Billy Walker, Dottie West, and I are going on a tour. Tex Ritter was going, but something came up and I'm taking his place. Our last show will be a benefit for the family of Cactus Jack Call in Kansas City. You remember our old deejay buddy who was killed in a car accident?

"Well, when I get back to Nashville, I promise you I'll be in church the next Sunday." Hawkshaw stood and circled the date of March 9, 1963, on a wall calendar.

The evening before they left, Patsy Cline helped Loretta Lynn hang drapes. Patsy had just replaced Kitty Wells as number-one female singer and Loretta had been voted "Most Promising Singer." "You're going to be number-one next year," Patsy predicted.

"Don't be silly," Loretta argued. "You'll be number-one for years to come."

After they hung the drapes, they went to Patsy's house to hear some tapes. As they listened, Patsy embroidered a tablecloth while her little boy, Randy, played on a rocking horse nearby. Before Loretta left at about midnight, Patsy gave her a red nightgown. They set a date to go shopping when the group returned from Kansas City.

Cowboy's son-in-law, Randy Hughes, flew Patsy, Cowboy, and Hawkshaw in his private Comanche plans. Dottie West and her husband went by car; Billy Walker flew commercial. The Monday after the show in Kansas City dawned cold, stormy, and rainy. Randy suggested they delay their flight home.

The Fateful Flight

While Dottie and Patsy breakfasted together in the hotel coffee shop, Patsy seemed eager to get back to her babies. "Why don't you ride home with us?" Dottie suggested. "No telling when your plane will go. Let the men fly. Billy Walker can take your place." Patsy agreed to do that and left to pack.

When Patsy returned to the lobby, her mind was changed. "Baby, ya'll go on. Even if we don't take off for a few hours, I can still beat you."

Dottie kept urging her to go in the car. "No, go on," Patsy insisted. "I'll be all right. If it's my time to go, I'll go."

Tuesday morning the Kansas City airport was locked in by fog, but by early afternoon, flights were cleared. Billy Walker boarded a commercial plane. At 2 p.m., Patsy, Cowboy, and Hawkshaw climbed into the single-engine Comanche with Randy.

At around 5 p.m. they stopped in Dyersburg, TN, for refueling as planned. Thunderstorms were rolling through the area. The Dyersburg airport manager advised them to stay on the ground. The three performers talked about leaving Randy and renting a car but finally decided to fly through the storms anyway, since they were so close to Nashville. They took off from Dyersburg at 6:07 p.m.

Wednesday morning at 3 a.m. Nashville time, Patsy's brother in Winchester, VA, stumbled into the kitchen to answer the phone. "I heard on the radio that a plane crashed with Patsy on board," a friend reported.

"Are you pulling a joke?" Sam replied angrily. "Patsy isn't on a plane."

Patsy's mother grabbed the phone. "Hold it. Patsy WAS on a plane!"

Later that morning Loretta Lynn began wondering why Patsy hadn't called her. They were supposed to go shopping. Just then the phone rang. It was Patsy's booking agent. His voice was shaking. "Loretta, Patsy and a whole bunch died in a plane crash."

Loretta didn't believe it. "Baloney! Patsy and me are goin' shoppin' this mornin'".

"Turn on your radio," the agent said.

Loretta did and heard the horrible truth.

Reports of a plane in trouble had started being announced at around 7 o'clock the evening before, about the time the group had been scheduled to land in Nashville. Search crews combed the dense woods in the area. About 6 a.m. a farmer and his son located the crash site on a ridge.

The plane had apparently sliced off the top of an oak while it was trying to land. Wreckage and bodies were strewn along a 250-foot stretch from the tree. Even before they found purses and wallets, rescuers identified the victims. A white belt emblazoned "Hawkshaw Hawkins" lay beside a black-and-white cowboy boot. A soft, gold slipper was identified as Patsy's. A *Flyer's Bible* was found under torn clothing. A hand-printed song titled *Boo Hoo Hoo* cried out the sad ending.

Adding pathos to the tragedy, record producer Don Pierce showed reporters Cowboy Copas' newly released album, *Beyond the Sunset.* Besides the title song it included *Family Reunion, The Wreck on the Highway,* and *A Picture from Life's Other Side.*

What Do We Say When We Lose Such Friends?

Family members were notified; funerals were scheduled. Cowboy, Randy, and Hawkshaw were buried in Nashville's Forest Lawn Cemetery. Patsy's remains were sent in a gold-trimmed casket to Winchester for burial. A simple, bronze plaque placed over her grave read:

VIRGINIA H. (PATSY CLINE) DICK
1932-1963
DEATH CANNOT KILL WHAT NEVER DIES

For a week Country-music fans streamed through Nashville's Forest Lawn Cemetery. At times the line of cars stretched five-miles long. Mountains of flowers covered the graves, both in Nashville and Winchester. During the week scores of radio stations broadcast songs by Cowboy, Hawkshaw, and Patsy, as well as by Opry star Jack Anglin, who had been killed on his way to Patsy's funeral in Virginia.

The Saturday-night memorial service before the Opry in Ryman Auditorium was something people never forgot.

"What do we say when we lose such friends?"pondered Opry manager Ott Devine. "We can reflect upon their contributions to all of us through entertainment and on their acts of charity and love. We can think of the pleasure they brought to the lives of millions and take some comfort in knowing that they found fulfillment in the time allotted to them. We can share the sorrow of their families and appreciate their loss . . . "

Devine asked everyone to stand and "join us for a moment of silent prayer in tribute to them."

"Thank you," he said after a moment. "Patsy, Cowboy, Hawkshaw, Jack, and Randy never walked on this stage without a smile. They would want us to keep on smiling . . . and to recall the happier occasions. I feel that I can speak for all of them when I say . . . let's continue in the tradition of the Grand Ole Opry."

The Jordainaires closed the tribute by singing *How Great Thou Art*.

The show went on. Roy Acuff struck up a fast fiddle tune. Minnie Pearl was next. Standing in the wings Minnie motioned to Roy for another minute to compose herself. When he waved her on, Minnie was still wiping her eyes as she rushed out on stage and shouted her familiar, down-home greeting, "Howdee, I'm jist so proud to be here!" A sea of handkerchiefs fluttered before her. A moment later she had the audience howling with laughter.

When Minnie reached the solace of the wings, she burst into tears again. "Oh, Lord," she cried, "we lost some good friends!"

On March 29, 1963, Texas Ruby Fox, a member of the Opry since 1933, died in a trailer fire.

Then it was "Gentleman" Jim Reeves.

An injury had cut short Jim's budding career in baseball. Turning to music he made it big with *Mexican Joe* and *Bimbo*.

His soft, soothing sound, similar to that of Eddie Arnold, gave a touch of velvet that fans loved who didn't appreciate the high, fast songs of Hank Williams, Faron Young, Webb Pierce, and others.

On July 31, 1964, Jim and Dean Manuel, Jim's road man-ager-pianist, were flying back from Arkansas. Just 20 miles south of Nashville their plane was caught in a thunderstorm and crashed near Brentwood in a wooded area. Jim was just 20 days short of his 41st birthday.

Many Country music luminaries had homes in Brentwood. Marty Robbins heard the plane's engine sputtering but had no idea his friends were in trouble. After the crash was confirmed,

Eddie Arnold scoured the area in a jeep. Carl Smith brought riding horses. Minnie Pearl, Stonewall Jackson, and others in the music business stayed in the woods all night.

By Saturday the crowds were so large, the police had to make radio broadcasts begging people to stay away. Tears and tension pervaded the Opry that night. Many entertainers requested prayer for Jim and Dean. Searchers finally stumbled on the fallen plane the next day. It was just 50 yards from a home. Both men lay dead in the mangled wreckage.

Occurring a little more than a year after Patsy Cline and her friends had been killed, this tragedy again plunged the music community into mourning. Massive crowds attended memorial services in Nashville and Jim's burial in his native Carthage, TX. Near his grave Jim's widow, Mary, set aside a two-acre memorial park with a life-sized statue of the singer standing on a monument. Workmen constructed a winding sidewalk leading to the grave. Part of the sidewalk was shaped like a guitar on which were inscribed the dates of Jim's birth and death and the words:

GENTLEMAN: JIM
PRODUCER: GOD

The seven deaths moved Jimmie Snow more than ever to start a church in Nashville. While he and Carol drove around looking for possible sites, another Opry friend, Ira Louvin, died tragically. He and his brother Charlie had been famous for their songs *Weapon of Prayer* and *The Family Who Prays*.

A New Church for Country-Music People

The Snows found a four-acre plot on Dickerson Road. They put up $600 for an option from their savings in evangelism. They spent $900 for renting 500 chairs, an organ, and a public-address system for the planned weeknight services.

Jimmie and Carol made radio and television appearances. The two Nashville newspapers ran feature stories on them. Opry friends arrived to sing during the evening services. Decisions to trust Christ were made almost every single night.

On the last day in September 1965 Jimmie announced the first Sunday-morning services. He anticipated at least a hundred people, but only 10 arrived. That included himself and Carol. By the end of October they had 23 members—enough for a charter as an Assemblies of God church.

Having long been back in Hank's good graces Jimmie stopped by to see his father.

"Are you serious about this church?" Hank called to Jimmie on his way out.

"Yes," Jimmie assured him. "But our option to buy the four acres on Dickerson Road is running out."

"How much is the price?" Hank asked.

"The balance is $39,400."

Hank wasted no words. "I'll lend the money. The church can pay me back over the next four years. Without interest."

Jimmie was overwhelmed. His father never had even been to hear him preach! "Yes, sir, thank you very much," was all Jimmie could say.

The land was purchased; building began. The new Evangel Temple sanctuary cost only $75,000 because the members did much of the work themselves. At Jimmie's instructions, it had good acoustics and a sloping floor like one might see at a treater.

To pay for the building the church issued bonds. Johnny Cash took $4,000 worth. Other entertainers pitched in until the issue was sold.

By 1968 attendance was up to 200. One of the first

Country-music couples to start attending regularly was Lefty and Alice Frizell, The son of a Texas oil driller, Lefty had placed four songs in the "Top Ten" in one year. This included his trademark, Always Late. Lefty withstood every invitation to accept Christ, but his wife, Alice, became a loyal member.

Billy Walker Gets a New Manager

The first really big performer to join the church was Billy Walker. Jimmie had known Billy since Dallas days when Billy and Hank Snow worked together on the Big D Jamboree.

The seventh of eight children from a poor West Texas farm family, Billy was only 4 when his mother died. "The crying woke me up," he recalls. "I asked, 'What's wrong?" They said, 'Mama died.' I went into the next room and saw them tying Mama's feet together. She had died in childbirth."

Billy's father worked in the oil fields. When Billy was 6, he and his two brothers were put in the Methodist Orphans Home in Waco. The matrons often whipped the children. When Billy and his brothers tried to run away, they were caught and beaten.

Their father remarried and brought the family together again in Clovis, NM. The elder Walker loved gospel-quartet singing and took Billy to singing conventions. Billy's first public singing was in a gospel quartet with his father, step-mother, and a family friend.

At 15 Billy won a talent contest and got his own show on KICA, Clovis. Later he worked as a front man for Hank Thompson. He then married a Texas girl and was hired for the Big D Jamboree. His manager put a Lone Ranger mask on him and billed him "The Traveling Texan, the Masked Singer of Country Songs." Billy hit big with *Anything Your Heart Desires*. During the next 20 years he landed 26 recordings in the "Top Ten."

From Dallas Billy moved to the Louisiana Hayride, where he worked with Hank Williams. One night Hank told Billy, "I want to get my life straightened out. I'm gonna do it."

The Ozark Jubilee with Red Foley in Springfield, MO, was next. In the early 1950s Billy and Red became close friends. At that time Red Foley was "Mr. Country Music", the first Country artist to sell a million records with his trademark gospel song, *Peace in the Valley*. When he sang *Shake a Hand,* Red could warm up the coldest audience. With *Peace in the Valley* and *Steal Away* He could turn a nightclub into a sanctuary of reverence.

But Red had no peace in his own heart. He had attended Georgetown Baptist College in Kentucky. His first wife, Pauline, died giving birth to their daughter, Betty. His second wife, Eva, gave him Shirley. Eva reportedly died of a broken heart after Red began seeing a nightclub singer. When Eva died, Red married the singer. His teen-aged daughter, Shirley, eloped with a young Nashville preacher named Pat Boone. Haunted by guilt over his second wife's death, Red tried to drown his misery with alcohol and pills. He overdosed on pills once and was saved from death only because he was taken to a hospital in time.

Billy Walker knew about Red's drinking, pill-taking, and heavy guilt, but at that time he didn't know how to help Red.

Billy joined the Opry in 1960 and recorded his smash hit, *Charlie's Shoes*. When he met preacher Jimmie Snow, he had a comfortable bank account, four beautiful daughters, a home near a golf course, and all the bookings he could deal with.

Billy and Jimmie Snow met for lunch at the Shoney's restaurant near Jimmie's home. As they talked, Billy confided that his family seldom went to church except on Easter. "My grandfather was a Methodist minister. When I was about 14, I accepted the Lord. But I got away from God after I started singing on the radio." Jimmie had heard it all before. So many Country entertainers had gone the path of Billy Walker.

"Jimmie, I've got success, money, everything the world thinks it takes to make you happy. But I'm in misery. Something more than this has to be out there."

Jimmie gave Billy his testimony. "If God can help me, I know He can help you."

"Just tell me how."

There in the booth Jimmie led Billy to spiritual renewal. He told Jimmie, "There are a lot of others like me. We've got to help them find Jesus."

Red Foley Finds "Peace in the Valley"

One of the friends Billy most wanted to help was Red Foley. "Mr. Country Music", as Red recently had been called by *Newsweek*, was now perhaps the best-loved and most enduring of all the Country artists. Red had dozens of hits under his belt. He had no known enemies; saint and sinner alike loved him.

When Red sang his all-time favorite hymn, *Peace in the Valley*, you almost could hear angel wings fluttering and the bells of heaven ringing.

In 1967 at the age of 57 Red was voted into the Country Music Hall of Fame along with deceased Jim Reeves. Although his red hair was lighter and his face showed wrinkles, he seemed to have the ability to go on forever as he made people laugh and cry. But those close to him wondered how much more drinking, chain-smoking, and nightly road shows his body could endure. Red said he had to keep going. "I need every dollar I can make," he told friends.

Red's son-in-law, Pat Boone, now was climbing the golden

stairs in Hollywood. Perhaps the fact that Red didn't know that Pat and Shirley's marriage was falling apart was best. Pat, who had been pastor of a church in Texas for a year and was known for his Mr. Clean, white-buck-shoes image, was breaking Shirley's heart.

Partying, drinking with the "beautiful people", and then attending church on Sunday, Pat had become a first-class hypocrite in Shirley's eyes. She tried to help him see where he was heading, but he kept making excuses about balancing religion with the real world. Shirley developed such an emotional reaction to Pat that she felt nauseous whenever he tried to either hold her hand or kiss her.

California businessman George Otis was the one who assured them that they could experience spiritual power. They actually could know God, walk in fellowship with Him, and sense the presence and power of the Holy Spirit. "God is alive today and can make you alive today if you will yield to Him," Otis assured them.

During the summer of 1968 Shirley took Otis's suggestions to "simply surrender yourself to the Lord" and found new direction and power for herself. For several more months Pat continued to struggle.

When Red Foley arrived to perform at Disneyland in Anaheim, CA, Pat and Shirley took the children to see "Grampa." Red had his grandchildren join him in singing *John Brown's Flivver Had a Puncture in Its Tire*. Afterward the family enjoyed a good time together laughing over old times and recalling some of Red's old movies with Tex Ritter.

Pat always enjoyed telling about the scene in which Red had gotten shot and, limping on one leg, had staggered off into the bushes. "Your Grampa," Pat told his kids," returned on camera a little later. He was still limping but on the OTHER leg." Red laughed heartily. Long ago he had forgiven Pat for eloping with his daughter. Sadly neither man could help the other spiritually at this time

On September 19 Red Foley, Billy Walker, and several other Opry members went to Terre Haute, IN. They did a Wednesday-afternoon matinee for 900 children. Red closed his act with the lively *Clap Your Hands*. Then the sponsors took the troupe out for food and drinks. Red noticed that Billy begged off the liquor.

Back at the auditorium Red went to Billy's dressing room. "Say, I've noticed that you're different, Billy. What happened?"

Billy related how he had been converted as a 14-year-old boy in Texas but had strayed away when he got into the music world. "I had to find out the hard way, Red, that success and money aren't everything."

"I know that," Red interjected.

Then Billy told him, "I asked the Lord to forgive me and I turned my life over to God, Red. Things sure have been different since then."

Red began telling Billy the pattern of his life. "I've done an awful lot I'm sorry for. Things I can't forget. I carry this heavy burden everywhere I go. When I go out on stage and make folks laugh and when I sing the hymns, the burden is still there. What can I do, Billy?"

Billy had a good idea what was worrying Red the most, but he didn't probe. "Red," he said as he placed a comforting hand on his friend's shoulder, "have you thought about asking the Lord to forgive you, to come into your heart and take that burden?"

Red brushed a hand through hair that was growing thin and sandy with age. He now was 58. "I've done an awful lot of things I regret."

"We all have, but the Lord is merciful. He'll forgive you if you just ask Him. You know He cared enough to die on the cross for your sins."

Red began sobbing, which was not unusual for the performer who could cry easily and make an audience cry. "OK, Billy, I'm ready. I meant it. I'm ready. Will you have a prayer with me?"

Red and Billy knelt in the dressing room while the audience waited. "Oh, Lord," Red sobbed, "You know how much I want to live a different life. Lord, you know I can't do it myself. Lord, forgive me. Come into my heart and help me, Please, Lord. I give it all over to you."

After Billy closed in prayer, they joined the others for the show. Red put on another marvelous performance. He sang *Old Shep*, which always brought the tears. Next was a recitation about a black couple whose dead baby was at the altar; the preacher conducting the funeral service was telling them that their baby was home with God.

Red ended with *Peace in the Valley*. He left the audience in tears.

Red walked offstage to talk with Billy Walker. "Old pal, I want to tell you I've never sung that song like I sang it tonight. There's peace in the valley for me. That's for real."

At midmorning the next day Red was found dead in bed. A United Airlines ticket for the 2:57 p.m. flight back to Nashville lay nearby.

Sally Foley, Red's third wife, waited at the Nashville airport. When Red didn't arrive as scheduled, she called his motel and was referred to the sheriff's office. He gave her the sad news.

The autopsy showed that Clyde Julian "Red" Foley had died of "massive, acute pulmonary edema", which Coroner Gordon Franke defined as water-logged lungs.

The Country-music community again was plunged into

mourning. Ralph Emery, WSM's top deejay, played nothing but Red Foley records on his program, Opry Stars. "Red gave me my biggest break," Emery said over the air. When they heard the news, many Opry personalities cried.

Red's funeral and burial services were held at 2 p.m. the following Sunday. More than 2,000, including all the big names from Opry and Country music in the Nashville area, overflowed the church in Madison where his black-veiled widow, Sally, at with her son, two daughters, and two step-daughters. Pat and Shirley Boone were there, Red's aged parents traveled there from Kentucky. Many other relatives were there as well.

Dr. Ira North read Psalm 23:

The Lord is my shepherd; I shall not want . . .
Yea, though I walk through the valley of the
    shadow of death,
I will fear no evil . . .

Then the Jordainaires sang the song Red had made famous:

There will be peace in the valley some day . . .
There'll be no sadness, no sorrow, no trouble I see
There will be peace in the valley for me.

"You don't weep alone," the preacher assured the grieving family. "Isn't it wonderful to have so many friends who care? And that is really that it is all about today. All of us here are trying to say simply that we care."

North then quoted one of Red's recitations:

Just remember that when you take the last
breath and go to the Great Beyond, all your

*belongings, all your earthly possessions will
then belong to someone else. But everything that
you are and everything that you have been will
be yours forever.*

At the graveside service Red's children hovered close to
Sally Foley. Pat Boone, still struggling to find spiritual victory,
noticed that Shirley was fully composed and steadying her
stepmother. Remembering the stormy past of the Foley family
and the sad death of Shirley's mother, Pat knew that his wife
was being undergirded with a power beyond herself.
The preacher intoned a prayer of commitment. Sally Foley
took a single red rose and placed it gently beside the grave. As
Red's body was slowly lowered into the ground, his family
and friends turned away sadly.
When Billy Walker later saw Shirley Boone, they talked
about her father. "There's something I should tell you," Billy
said. Then he recounted his experience with Red in Terre
Haute between shows and the prayers in the dressing room.
"Your daddy died with peace," he assured her. "He had the
same peace you and I have in the Lord."

Chapter 6
Stars Reborn

Evangel Temple soon became known as the church for
Country-music personalities

Jimmie and Carol Snow were insiders within the music
culture. They knew the language and rhythm of Country
music. Jimmie preached a gospel Country artists could understand. Carol could make the organ talk and the choir move. A
string band with cymbals and drums kept toes tapping. An
exciting freshness made church something to look forward to
each Sunday. Six to eight persons were converted every week.

Elaine Walker, the daughter of Ernest Tubb, was married to
songwriter Wayne Walker. As kids backstage at the Opry
Jimmie and Elaine had played together.

The Walkers' son attended Vacation Bible School. Elaine
went to see her youngster perform at the graduation exercises
and became a Christian and a loyal member of Evangel
Temple.

Eddie Miller: "Now I've Gotta
Rewrite All My Songs"

Barbara Miller and her songwriter husband, Eddie, also
were reached through a song by their daughter, Pam, at the

church. The next morning at work Eddie raced up the stairs to see his good friend, Biff Collie, who had an office in the same building. For several years Biff had been witnessing to Eddie. T. Tex Tyler also had been telling Eddie that Christ could set him free from the bottle.

"Gotta tell you something, Biff," Eddie shouted. "Gotta tell you that the Lord changed my life yesterday. I couldn't wait to get to that altar. I thought Jimmie Snow was going to preach for two months."

"Well, praise God!" Biff declared. "This is really good news."

"Yeah, and I've thrown out all my whiskey. Now I've gotta rewrite all my songs."

Two days later Biff and Eddie heard that Tex Tyler was dying from cancer. They phoned Tex. Eddie told him about the miracle in his life. "I can go now, Eddie," Tex said joyfully. "Ever since I was saved, I dreamed it would happen to you."

Eddie Miller's big song had been *Please Release Me*. After he became a Christian, he wrote, *Please Release Me from My Sins*. He and his daughter also penned several gospel songs based on sermons they heard Jimmie Snow preach. *Crumbs from the Table* was inspired by Jimmie's message on the rich man and Lazarus. *The Last Altar Call* was based on Jimmie's invitation to accept Christ.

Connie Smith: Newborn Christian

Jimmie and Carol Snow now were being seen on WSM-TV every Sunday morning. The station gave them free air time with the understanding that Opry talent would "guest" on the program. Emceed by Jimmie and featuring the biggest names in Country music, Gospel Country had the second-largest television-viewing audience in Nashville.

One of the first Gospel Country shows featured Connie Smith, born Constance June Meador. A hundred-pound package of honey-blonde dynamite, Connie was the idol of thousands of young women. They didn't know her heart was breaking.

As a girl in West Virginia she and her father had listened to the Opry. When she was barely 5, she told her father confidently, "Someday I'm gonna sing on that Grand Ole Opry."

Her father died and her mother remarried a bulldozer operator with eight children. This increased the family size to 16. They moved to Ohio and became active in a church where Connie sang with her brothers and sisters. She was a married woman at 22 when Opry's Bill Anderson heard her at a talent contest in Columbus, OH. "You're pretty good," he said. "Come to Nashville and I'll get you on the Saturday midnight show at Ernest Tubbs' Record Shop."

In Nashville Connie sang before a huge crowd. After she stepped down, a round-faced man with thinning hair handed her a note: "Stick with it, no matter what. You've got what it takes." The note, signed Loretta Lynn, had been delivered by Loretta's husband, Mooney. Connie returned home in high spirits.

Bill Anderson brought her back to Nashville for a demo record. Chet Atkins heard it and signed her for RCA. Her first recording *Once a Day*, became the number-one Country song and stayed on the peak for almost three months. The next year, 1965, *Billboard* voted Connie female vocalist of the year.

More hits followed: *Ain't Had No Lovin', The Hurtin's All Over, and Ribbon of Darkness*, among others. The songs reflected much of Connie's life. Her first marriage had broken up. She had two young sons. Her second marriage now was floundering. Also she had been making weekly visits to a psychiatrist before Jimmie Snow invited her to sing on "Gospel

Country."

She sang *In the Garden.* Near the end of the show Jimmie noticed her in tears as she sat on the far side of the studio. After he signed, he walked over and asked, "May I be of any help?"

"I really don't know why I'm crying."

"Perhaps God is speaking to you."

She told him about her problems and added, "I just can't seem to come up to God's standards."

Opening his New Testament Jimmie read about Jesus' sacrificial death on the cross. "You never can be good enough for God," he said. "None of us can. That's why Jesus died on the cross for our sins. If you'll ask Him, He'll forgive you and make you the person God wants you to be . . . Would you like to pray the sinner's prayer and ask Jesus to come into your heart?"

"Oh, yes," Connie murmured softly.

They prayed while the other performers and the studio audience looked on.

Becoming a Christian didn't save Connie's second marriage, but the experience in the studio changed her life. She became an active member of Evangel Temple and sang for many evangelists across the country and for the Presidential Prayer Breakfast.

At Evangel Temple she met and married Marshall Haynes, a committed Christian and a telephone installer. "I've found that God still cares for me after two broken marriages," she told the congregation. "Even if I knew there wasn't a heaven for the peace that God has given me through Jesus Christ I'd still want to be a Christian."

For the next few years Connie boldly gave her testimony at performances, including the Opry. She was so outspoken that Opry officials asked her to refrain. One man at a concert became so upset at her testimony that he yelled, "Sing the songs, lady." Connie eased up. Not that she wasn't willing to declare her faith, but, "I don't want people to think I tricked them into going to church. My main goal is still to be a Christian and serve the Lord. I am just going about that differently."

The Skeeter Davis Story

One of the many stars who encouraged Connie Smith was Skeeter Davis. Another Cinderella singer, Skeeter also had her share of heartaches.

Born Mary Frances Penick, the oldest of seven children, Skeeter grew up in the poverty of Dry Ridge, KY. Her father had a drinking problem; the family survived on welfare. "Mary Frances flits around like a skeeter," her grandfather observed. "Skeeter" stuck as her permanent nickname.

When Skeeter turned 2, her beloved grandfather was murdered on Christmas Day. Every Christmas after that her mother cried over the tragedy.

As a little girl, Skeeter listened to the Carter Family on the Mexican border station and the Grand Ole Opry over WSM. Like Connie Smith, Patsy Cline, and so many others, she dreamed of someday singing on the Opry and meeting the stars.

Skeeter sang to relatives and neighbors, who gave her nickels and dimes. Once she performed for a peddler, who tossed her candy. "I wanted to please people and have them like me more than anyone else," Skeeter recalls.

In high school she and her best friend, Betty Jack Davis, teamed together as the "Davis Sisters." They got a radio show and in 1953, when Skeeter was only 21, their RCA recording of *I Forgot More than You'll Ever Know,* climbed to the Top

Ten. In August of that year their car collided with another head-on. The crash left Betty Jack dead and Skeeter seriously injured.

Skeeter required months to recover physically and emotionally, but by 1954 she was back on the circuit. She performed with Hank Snow, Eddie Arnold, and Elvis Presley. She joined the Opry in 1959 and married WSM's most popular deejay, Ralph Emery. In 1963 she became the first pure Country female to sell more than a million records with the hit, *End of the World*. That year her marriage with Ralph Emery hit bottom. The following year she was divorced.

Skeeter never liked to talk about her relationship with the deejay. All she would say was that "the courtship was beautiful and the marriage a disaster. We were very incompatible."

The breakup sent her life into another tailspin. Through reared in Sunday school and converted at 18, Skeeter, like so many Country musicians, had put her career ahead of God. Realizing her mistake, she began asking around for a good church.

Several show-business friends recommended Forest Hills. "The preacher has a heart for Country entertainers," they told her.

She found the church but was crying so much over her divorce that she sat in the parking lot until everybody left the church. The next Sunday she did the same thing.

One Sunday Pastor Bob Daughtery approached Skeeter in her car and noticed that she was crying. "Can I do something to help?" he asked.

"Just pray for me," she sobbed.

Finally drying her tears, she went inside. From then on she attended three times every week. But three years passed before she gained "any victory" in her heart. "I felt totally lost, sad, depressed, and unloved. I felt as though nobody loved me except Pastor Bob and his wife." Finally she realized that the real blockage was in herself. "I wasn't willing to turn over my life one-hundred percent to the Lord."

Suspended from the Opry

When Skeeter was in a Nashville shopping center, she saw police arrest several long-haired "Jesus People" on a complaint of harassment. A group calling themselves "Christ Is the Answer" had set up a meeting tent on a downtown lot and in the shopping area had been distributing invitations and gospel tracts.

On stage at the Opry that night Skeeter mentioned the incident. "They've arrested 15 people just for telling other people that Jesus loves them. That really burdened my heart, so I thought I'd sing you all this song." Then she led the audience in *Amazing Grace*.

The Opry had an unwritten policy that entertainers were not to use the stage as a platform for personal opinion on controversial religious or political subjects. The police complained to the Opry management. After hearing a tape the Opry management suspended Skeeter from the Opry until further notice. As for Skeeter, she sang with the Christ Is the Answer young people and invited them to stay a while at her farm outside Nashville. Then she left for road concerts.

After 15 months the Opry lifted her suspension. "Sometimes you can be too righteous," Skeeter says. She added, "The Lord taught me that my ego wasn't so big. I had been used to traveling first class and staying at the best hostels. When I went off the Opry, my earnings dropped way down. I had to stay in homes and live as an ordinary Christian."

After she returned to the Opry, she heard that her grandfather's murderer was out of prison and set out to find him. She located 71-year-old Dilver Webster living just a few miles from where her grandfather had been killed. The ex-con was now an old man suffering from cancer, but when Skeeter arrived, he recognized her immediately and hugged her joyfully.

"I've been wanting to see you for years," he said. "My wife and I have all of your record albums."

He drew back and looked off into the distance as if he were seeing a vision from the past. "You'll never know how much I regret what happened. I've had to live with it for more than 40 years."

"You've paid your debt, Mr. Webster," Skeeter assured him. "I forgive you and the Lord will forgive you also."

After more talk Skeeter left. She felt happy that she had found the old man and lifted his burden.

She still bears the nickname "Skeeter", although on stage she's a more a blond, green-eyed butterfly as she flits about in a long gown of many colors, with long hair flying.

The old gospel quartet song, *I'll Fly Away*, is one of her favorites.

To some Skeeter gives the impression of a gadfly, but when the occasion demands, she can be decisive and stand for her convictions.

Once after arriving in a town in Illinois, she learned she had been booked into a nightclub. She immediately told the manager, "There's been a mistake. I don't sing where alcohol is sold."

The man got huffy; Skeeter called her agent. "I can't work this place," she said, but he urged her to go ahead "just this once, since you're already here."

"No," Skeeter declared. "I won't sing and have drunks hollering at me."

The manager retuned. "We have a contract and you're going to sing. I'm calling you up and you'd better be ready."

He walked to the front and announced Skeeter. She went on stage and said, "I'm sorry, but there's been a misunderstanding. Please understand I don't say this with condemning spirit. I really love people, but I don't entertain in nightclubs. You may not agree with me and that's your privilege, but I wouldn't want to be singing in a club when my Lord returns." Then she walked off the stage.

"We'll sue you for every cent you've got," the manager fumed.

"They crucified my Jesus," Skeeter said and left.

The club didn't sue; her testimony was the talk of the town.

In recent years Skeeter has become a big attraction overseas. At one appearance in Sweden she sang gospel songs and gave her witness before 40,000 people. In Africa she made an agreement with promoters to give a Country-music show if they'd allow her to close with her testimony and an evangelistic appeal. Singing before crowds of 25,000 she saw many Africans become born again.

"When I became a Christian at 18," Skeeter recalls, "I wanted to go to Africa as a missionary. If the Lord tells you that, then go. If it's just you, wait. I'm glad I waited."

She continues to sing on the Opry. I saw her there recently, her hair pushed back with ribbons, curls swinging below her shoulders above an old-fashioned dress, smiling, casting glances across the crowd, waving and curtsying as she entered the stage.

Skeeter has not remarried. She lives in suburban Brentwood near some Opry friends. Her house is something of a menagerie with seven dogs, assorted cats, a dove, and an ocelot. "I love them all," she says. "I love everybody."

Jeannie of "Harper Valley" Fame

A dear friend of Skeeter's is Jeannie C. Riley, her sister in Christ. The story of how the sassy, sarcastic, Sexy "Harper Valley PTA" girl in flouncy miniskirt and shiny white boots became a Christian and changed her showbiz image still is being told in Country-music circles.

Jeannie Carolyn Stephenson, the second of three sisters, grew up on a cotton farm in north Texas. As a little girl she rode the back of her mother's cotton sack into the field; when she was older, she chopped and picked cotton. On Sundays she went with her family to the Nazarene church where her Grandfather Moore preached.

"I always thought of Grandfather as Moses sent to lead our family out of the wilderness of sin," Jeannie says, She went to the church altar twice without surrendering her life. "I didn't really understand the plan of salvation."

At age 10 she was stricken with rheumatic fever. For entertainment her parents put an old radio beside her bed. Listening to the Carter Family, Patsy Cline, Hank Snow, Ernest Tubb, and other greats, she learned many songs by heart. She really wanted to grow up and marry Elvis Presley. When she realized the impossibility of that, she locked herself in the bathroom and cried.

She recovered from the fever. At Anson High School she was a majorette and voted "Most Popular Girl." At 16 she made her first stage appearance as she sang Marty Robbins' hit, *I Couldn't Keep from Crying*. She walked offstage and hoped they'd call her to sing again. Show business had gotten into her blood. From there she only had to make a short step to performing for a monthly amateur night held in a country schoolhouse.

At 18 Jeannie married her high-school sweetheart, Mickey

Riley. A few months later she graduated at the top of her class.

Connie Smith released her *Once a Day*. People told Jeannie, "You belt it out like Connie. You can make it in show business."

She saved her money to visit Nashville and cut a demo record. A photographer did a photo layout of her in the only dress she had to wear—a bridesmaid's gown she had worn to the wedding of a friend back home.

When the demo didn't work out, she went home discouraged.

Weldon Myrick, a fellow Texan and a friend in Nashville, urged her and Mickey to move to Nashville if they really intended to "get in the business."

In the summer of 1966 Jeannie, Mickey, and their new baby chugged into Opry City in an old car pulling a trailer loaded with their possessions.

Mickey got a job at a service station. Carrying her baby, Kim, Jeannie trudged from office to office along Music Row. She told producers, "Please listen to my demo." She budgeted $15 a week for groceries and on layaway bought dresses from discount stores. Every morning she woke up with one thought: *Maybe this is the day.* After two years she was still waiting for the big break.

A songwriter friend, Jerry Chestnut, hired her as a secretary for $50 a week. "I was the worst typist he ever had," Jeannie admits. "He gave me the job out of kindness so I could be close to people on Music Row."

Plantation Records' producer Shelby Singleton was looking for a fresh voice to record a message written by Tom T. Hall. When he heard one of Jeannie's demos, he exclaimed, "That's the girl!"

He called Jeannie and offered her a contract, but she hesitated. Plantation was a new and unknown company. Shouldn't she wait for a better opportunity? "Take it," friends encouraged. She did.

On July 25, 1968, she cut *Harper Valley PTA*. It was a hot, humid day in Nashville. At 2 the next morning Ralph Emery aired the song over his all-night radio show on WSM. The switchboard lit up: "Who was that girl?" "Play it again, Ralph."

Before she'd even left the studio, Jeannie was certain *Harper Valley* would be a hit. She rushed home to phone her mother. "I've just cut the next number-one single in the country. I'll sell a million," The next night she called back. "Forget what I said about *Harper Valley* selling a million. It'll sell three million!"

Sales of the song about the widow Johnson socking it to the hypocritical Harper Valley PTA exploded. A week later sales neared the million mark. Jeannie quit her secretarial job and went on the road.

In miniskirt and white boots she played the Flamingo Hotel in Las Vegas, appeared at the Hollywood Palace with Bing Crosby, and hit the biggest show spots in-between. Within six months she had won a stack of awards and was back home for "Jeannie C. Riley Day" with Texas Governor Preston Smith honoring her.

A press release described Jeannie as:

a bouncing, bubbling, intrigue of mirth with the beguiling charmer of a child, She laughs easily, flits around the room like a skittery butterfly, asks questions with the naivete of a five-year-old and constantly flips her waist-length shining brown locks over her shoulder.

She gives the impression of a vivacious child

until she steps in front of a microphone. Then
with the aplomb of a seasoned pro, she deepens
her tones . . . and turns on the sexiest grit heard
in ages.

Another release called her:

the sexiest and hottest item to hit the
entertainment scene since Peyton Place's
first illegitimate birth shattered the television
media.

Catapulted into a dazzling new lifestyle with a beautiful home and chauffeured cars, Jeannie became the center of attention at parties. Important people asked her for autographs. Entertainment personalities treated her as thought she were an equal. All of this was quite different from the high-school girl in Anson, TX, and the demure secretary in Nashville.

Without realizing what was happening she started changing. "Producers and agents insisted that I live that sassy, sex-pot image, rejecting the old values," she recalls. "It was something I fell, or was dragged into—not something I really felt. I was forced into a role that wasn't me but a masquerade. I didn't realize it then, but Satan was trying to decimate my life."

Mickey, still working at the service station, became "Mr. Jeannie C. Riley." The marriage couldn't stand the strain of Jeannie's success; they divorced. "This never would have happened," Jeanie said later, "if we'd stayed in church and had known the Lord."

Her dizzy whirl latest almost four years until she entered the hospital in exhaustion. "I was miserable, self-critical, and impatient with myself and life in general. I didn't like the person I'd become."

Jeannie's sister, Helen, gave her a copy of *The Living Bible*. Jeannie would have preferred a Gothic novel. At Helen's urging, however, Jeannie began reading the Bible and found it interesting and absorbing.

A friend brought her Pat Boone's book, *A New Song*. Many of Pat's experiences mirrored her own: a greenhorn falling in with a crowd having standards different from those by which she had been reared. Pat's deliverance and the healing of his and Shirley's marriage had impressed her.

She heard about Connie Smith finding God and a new life. One night backstage she talked with Connie, who was wearing a glittering diamond cross around her neck. "That's so beautiful," Jeannie said. Without a word Connie removed the cross and placed it around her friend's neck. The gesture made a tremendous impact on Jeannie, who began yearning for the same Christian love evident in Connie's life.

Jeannie started attending Forest Hills Baptist Church, where Skeeter Davis and several other performers were then worshiping. On the road she hunted up churches to visit.

One Sunday morning in April 1972 the "Harper Valley" girl went to Forest Hills in a low mood. A clear thought came: *Jeannie, if you don't turn to God now, you never will.* When Pastor Daughtery closed his sermon with an invitation to accept Christ, she walked forward to share her decision with the congregation. "I've never really trusted the Lord until then," Jeannie says. "I'd believed about Him, but I hadn't put my life totally into His hands. When I did that, everything began to change."

Her self-criticism disappeared; she accepted herself and stopped demanding too much. Her nervousness and exhaustion were gone. When impatient and frustrated, she would pray and become calm. Even her dress changed; she traded her "Harper Valley" miniskirt for more modest clothing.

She replaced her risque lyrics with gospel songs and songs of the heart. Her nightclub performances stopped.

Most important of all, she and Mickey began rebuilding their relationship. In 1975 they were remarried with daughter Kim serving as their flower girl.

During performances Jeannie began casually slipping in words of testimony. One night she told about her remarriage to Mickey. Afterward, a big, burly man approached. towering above her, he said gently, "Jeannie, would you pray for me and my ex-wife? Things haven't been right since we divorced. You told about how you remarried your husband. Would you pray that the same thing might happen to us?"

Fans began urging her to put her experience in a book. She did—with painstaking honesty. *From Harper Valley to the Mountain Top*—also the title of a gospel song—warmly chronicles her return to the faith of her preacher grandfather, W.R. Moore.

Her musical group, "Red River", supports her love of bluegrass, traditional Country, and rhythm-and-blues gospel. Daughter Kim Riley Coyle, who sings with Jeannie, bears her mother's entrancing beauty.

Jeannie and husband Mickey now make their home in Franklin, TN, a small town set in the rolling countryside south of Nashville. Jeannie jokingly refers to herself as "Jeannie C. Riley Riley" since she remarried Mickey.

She continues to do the Opry and make tours. Young people often are the first to rush forward for autographs "which may mean," Jeannie says, "that I'm still a youth at heart." Young or old, she says, "God wants me to be a witness for Him. He gave me all the talents I have."

Chapter 7
"Hello, I'm Johnny Cash"

The simple greeting from the big, craggy-faced man with weathered skin and brooding eyes is enough to make this audience—any audience—explode in applause.

Country music's legendary "Man in Black" opens another show. Talking or singing in sepulchral tones, with a quavering voice aptly described as "sounding like gravel dripping from hot molasses", Johnny Cash is one Country entertainer who can perform anywhere successfully.

He's equally at home in a casino supper club in Atlantic City as he is before network TV cameras, on a crusade platform with Evangelist Billy Graham, performing at a maximum-security prison, on a stage in Eastern Europe (44,000 Czech fans bought out the Winter Sports Hall in Prague, Czechoslovakia, a month in advance for one of his concerts), and anywhere else he's called to entertain.

The most respected performer in Country music, he's also the most enduring superstar Country artist.

Said the *Wichita Eagle*:

Johnny Cash is an institution. Criticize one of his concerts? Are you kidding?

Observed the *Philadelphia Daily News:*

*It doesn't matter how much musical fashions
change or how often he appears. Johnny Cash never
overstays his welcome. He remains the same.*

Johnny has been on more *Country Music* magazine covers
than any other performer. For his 25th anniversary in the profession *Country Music* put out a special edition and proclaimed "Johnny Cash is the longest-running superstar."
Obviously a wealthy man, he owns song-publishing houses
in the Nashville suburb of Hendersonville, commands top dollar for appearances, and sells millions of records. You can buy
Johnny Cash watches, silver patches, tote bags, mugs, and
even bells. In the Country Music Hall of Fame Museum in
Nashville you can see more authentic memorabilia.

"There is no person in the world whom [Ruth and I] love
more," says Billy Graham. Youth for Christ International
named Johnny "Man of the Year" for helping young people.
He attends both Baptist and Pentecostal churches and has an
honorary doctorate in humanities from Gardner-Webb College,
a Southern Baptist school in North Carolina.

Beloved by Prisoners

Many performers owe their first big break to Johnny Cash.
The Statler Brothers were virtual unknowns when Johnny
had them open his show in Virginia before he had even heard
them sing. After they returned home, he called them for another show, then another and another. With only a handshake to
seal the agreement, they began an eight-year relationship. The
Statlers have had the top Country variety show on television.
Kris Kristofferson is "sure I would never have been a per-

former were it not for Johnny Cash."

Johnny was "one of the first to befriend" Larry Gatlin when he "came to Nashville, the first to take an interest in my old homemade songs. The first to put me on national TV and the first to come bringing gifts to my son, whom we named Joshua Cash Gatlin."

However, no group loves the "Man in Black" more than do the prisoners for whom he often performs. They know about his brushes with the law and his battle with drugs. They know that he is a survivor and a victor—one who understand and offers hope. That's why Gary Mark Gilmore, during his last hours before execution at Utah State Prison, called Johnny Cash and asked him to sing *Amazing Grace*.

"The Hand of God Was Never Off Me"

Perhaps *Amazing Grace,* written by John Newton after the hard-drinking, profane, slave trader found God, best describes the climb of Johnny Cash from the pit of despair to the pinnacle of glory. The record shows that Johnny has more lives than 10 cats. For seven years he wrecked every car he ever had, totaled two Jeeps and a camper, overturned two tractors and a bulldozer, sank two boats in separate accidents on a lake, jumped from a truck just before it went over a 600-foot cliff in California, brawled and incurred permanent scars, and many times drove himself into a wild frenzy with drugs.

Yet when the raging voices quieted, he always heard the "still, small voice" whispering, *I am your God. I love you. I am waiting.*

"The hand of God," Johnny says, "was never off me." In all his wanderings he could never escape the "hound of heaven" which pursued him from his childhood.

As a young boy Johnny tapped his toes in the schoolhouse

revivals to the rhythm of guitars, mandolins, and banjos. He sang *Shall We Gather at the River?* during baptisms at the Blue Hole. At age 12 he was converted. "A beautiful peace came over me that night. I felt brand-new." He felt a touch of heaven when he put his cheek against his dying brother Jack's lips and heard him whisper, "I'm going to a beautiful city . . . I can hear the angels singing."

Arkansas Traveler

Then, like many other young men, he slipped from his home moorings and began to drink while he was in the service. Stationed in Germany in the early 1950s he joined a country band of fellow soldiers. "We were pretty rough," he admits, "but I don't think I ever enjoyed picking and singing so much."

He stopped drinking after he returned home and married Vivian Liberto, a Catholic girl. He didn't argue with Vivian about the requirement of her religion to rear the children Catholic. In fact when he was home, he usually took them to his wife's church.

As a young married man Johnny got a job selling appliances in Memphis. He spent more time listening to the radio than he did knocking on doors. Without any professional experience he applied for a deejay job in Mississippi. The station manager sent him back to Memphis to attend broadcasting school. There he became friends with two music-loving mechanics, Marshall Grant and Luther Perkins.

Their first request to sing was from a Pentecostal church just north of Memphis. "What are we gonna wear?" Luther asked. After he thought about it for a minute, Johnny replied, "Why don't we just wear black, 'cause black's best for church?" It's been black for Johnny Cash ever since.

They sang *Belshazzar*, a song Johnny wrote based on a sermon he had heard from the Book of Daniel. Johnny didn't feel comfortable because he hadn't been to church in a while, but he appreciated the loud *amens.*

He heard that Elvis Presley, the young, respectful Country singer from Mississippi, had made a recording for Sam Phillips at Sun Records in Memphis. Johnny camped outside Sam's office until the manager agreed to hear an audition. "OK, I'm gonna take a chance on you, Cash," Phillips said. "Let's hope you sell."

Johnny recorded a railroad ballad called *Hey, Porter*, and the tear-jerker, *Cry, Cry, Cry*, which he had written. Sam sent advance discs to deejays. Young Johnny Cash soon was being heard on stations across the Mid-South.

Calls for performances started arriving. Carl Perkins, a West Tennessean, joined Johnny, Marshall, and Luther. Carl reminded Johnny of his dead brother, Jack, who had wanted to be a preacher. Elvis Presley and a new talent from Louisiana, Jerry Lee Lewis, worked with them. Johnny, Carl, Elvis, and Jerry often harmonized together on hymns.

Johnny, Marshall, and Luther left to join the Louisiana Hayride on KWKH, Shreveport. Johnny found the atmosphere exhilarating and the crowds noisy and enthusiastic. Backstage, whiskey and beer flowed freely. "Snuff Queens" available for the night fluttered among fans asking for autographs. Despite the temptations around him Johnny walked the line.

He spent his first night away from home after he performed in Shreveport. The next morning, Sunday, Johnny and his two music pals headed for Gladewater, TX. They kept having to slow down to let cars turn in to churches along the highway. "We ought to go to church," Johnny said.

"Yeah, yeah, I hear you," Marshall agreed.

"If you want me to stop somewhere, say the word."

They never stopped. Johnny didn't realize it at the time, but he was starting a pattern of missing church. For many years this kept him from fellowship with other Christians.

When Johnny hit with *Folsom Prison Blues* and *I Walk the Line,* his career zoomed into high gear. From the Hayride, he moved to the Grand Ole Opry and made guest appearances on national television and took long road tours. By 1958 he had performed in every state in the union as well as in Carnegie Hall, the Hollywood Bowl, the London Palladium, and cities in Europe and the Far East.

"Why Would a Man Like You Let a Little [Pill] . . . Destroy His Life?"

During a long roadtrip with several Opry artists, one of the performers gave him a little white pill when he became sleepy. He soon was wide awake and alert. From that time he needed amphetamines to stay up. By 1960 he was hooked, nervous, and irritable. On brief trips home he couldn't sleep and walked the floor as he tried to wear off the pills.

Four daughters in quick succession kept his wife, Vivian, tied down. As the babies arrived, she fought against the long trips that kept her husband away from home. She began hating the career which was robbing her of Johnny's companionship.

In 1961 they moved to California, with Johnny vowing to do better. He rededicated his life to Christ and joined the Avenue Community Church in Ventura. He tried to beat the drugs but couldn't. He'd stagger in the house and fuss at Vivian and the girls.

His family grew to fear him. When he began to rant and yell, Vivian would call his pastor, Floyd Gresset, who would haul Johnny to a ranch hideout and keep him off drugs. Johnny would go back on the road again with good intentions but return hooked. In 1966 Vivian gave up and filed for divorce.

Johnny headed for Nashville.

He began working with the Statler Brothers and the Carter Family. Maybelle and Ezra Carter, loving him like the son they never had, gave him a key to their house. Sometimes he'd lose it, arrive home crazed from drugs and drink, and kick the door down. June Carter started throwing his pills away. Sometimes he was glad, sometimes angry. She kept saying, "Johnny, I intend to help you, whether you like it or not. God has His eyes on you." But he always knew where to get more.

Stories of the wild and irresponsible antics of Johnny Cash kept the Nashville gossip line humming. Many of the stories were true. He had canceled out on a couple of promoters and left them to face bankruptcy. He had painted motel rooms black. He had broken down motel doors, sawed the legs off furniture and beds, tied door knobs together in the night, sounded fire alarms, and turned baby chicks loose in corridors.

One night Johnny appeared on the Opry when he was in bad shape. The band had struck up a tune, but he couldn't remove his mike from its stand. In a fit of irrational anger he threw down the mike stand, picked it up, and dragged it to the edge of the stage. Then, oblivious to glass shattering over the stage and into the audience, he began popping the colored footlights. The Opry managed pulled him aside and said sadly, "We can't use you on the Opry anymore, John."

Johnny responded by jumping into his car and driving recklessly along rain-slick streets through a residential neighborhood. Crying and shaking he careened around corners on two wheels until the car went out of control and crashed into some trees. He totaled the car and climbed out with a broken jaw and nose.

Leaving the Carters he moved in with singer Waylon Jennings. Johnny tried hiding his pills from Waylon—to no avail. He decided to buy a house around Old Hickory Lake where Red Foley, Roy Acuff, and several other entertainers then lived. Down by a cove he stopped in front of the oddest residence he had ever seen. The building was at least 200-feet long with four big, 35-foot-round rooms—one over the other at each end of the house.

The house was set on a solid rock foundation. Johnny saw in it a symbol of rebuilding his life on the sure Rock of Ages. When the man working at the house said he was building it for himself, Johnny told contractor Braxton Dixon, "No, this is my house!" Johnny bought the place.

The new house didn't help. In October 1967 Johnny was arrested on a drug charge in Lafayette, GA, and locked in a cell. The next morning Sheriff Ralph Jones had him brought to the office.

Sheriff Jones looked sadly at the star, who was turning into a derelict. "Tell me, Mr. Cash," he said solemnly. "Why would a man like you, at the top of his profession, let a little thing like this [he held up a pill] destroy his life?"

An uncomfortable silence hung in the room. The lawman dropped his voice. "Mr. Cash, I'm not angry at you, just deeply hurt. I want you to know that my wife and I have followed your career for more than 10 years. We've bought every record you put out. You probably have no better fans than us. We've always loved you, and we're hurt."

Johnny had never felt so miserable and low.

"Here are your pills. Take them and go. It will be your decision to destroy yourself or save your life."

"Sheriff," Johnny finally said, "I give you my word that I'll never take another one." Then he walked outside and threw the pills on the ground.

Johnny and June

Johnny drove back to Nashville and told June Carter about the experience. She made an appointment for him to see Dr. Nat Winston, a psychiatrist and also Tennessee's commissioner of mental health.

Johnny made it through the first night. The next day he found a bottle of amphetamines and swallowed a handful. He got on a tractor and drove it into the lake. As he was crawling out of the ice-cold water, his contractor friend, Braxton Dion, appeared. Close behind were June and Dr. Winston.

June and the psychiatrist took him into the house and put him to bed. "I've seen a good many like you," Nat Winston said solemnly. "Many didn't make it. There isn't much hope for you unless you get God's help."

June, Maybelle, and Ezra Carter moved into Johnny's house and slept in sleeping bags downstairs to keep the pill-pushers away. Another friend sat beside his bed on the first night. An old drinking buddy managed to get past the first-floor guard and into the room. "Nurse" June ran him off with a butcher knife.

Johnny cried and prayed. His days and nights were filled with nightmares. He suffered excruciating cramps and hallucinations. At times he turned wild as he leaped about, knocked over furniture, and jerked up carpet. After four weeks of "cold turkey" he believed the battle wa won.

In November of that year he and June visited the First Baptist Church of Hendersonville. The pastor, Courtney Wilson, preached on "Jesus, the Living Water."

"I'm going to drink of that living water," Johnny told June. He went out and performed his first concert since he spent the night in the Georgia jail.

Carl Perkins, who had rejoined Johnny that year, had

become a slave to alcohol and was trying to fight his own way back to sobriety. After a show in San Diego, CA, Carl got drunk again. The next day the group stopped the bus to have a picnic near a beach. Carl, still hung over, began crying that he was dying. June pointed to the miracle in Johnny's life. "Call on God," she urged. "Let Him help you the way he did Johnny."

They got off the bus and left Carl in his bunk. After a while Johnny went to check on Carl and found him standing up holding a bottle of whiskey. Tears streamed down his face. "I've quit, John," he declared. "If God could help you quit, He can do it for me."

Carl walked out to the surf and threw the bottle in the ocean. Above the roar of the waves they could hear Carl praying, "God, have mercy! Help me!" He never took another drink.

After finding deliverance Carl wrote a song, *Daddy Sang Bass*, about family life as he and Johnny had known it as boys and about the hope of spending eternity in the family circle. The song included a line about Johnny's long-dead brother, Jack: "Me and little brother will join right 'n there." The song became a huge hit.

During his bad days Johnny had given many concerts in prisons. Now with a new song in his heart he had a message that truly could set prisoners free. In 1968 he went back to Folsom Prison with his old pastor friend, Floyd Gressett, and recorded an album with the Statler Brothers, Marshall, Luther, and June Carter. Johnny's deacon father also went along for the experience, The hardened prisoners were overwhelmed by Johnny's testimony. Numerous ones accepted Christ.

The Carters had become family to Johnny. He brought his four girls—Roseanne, Kathleen, Cindy, and Tara—from California to visit Mother Maybelle, Ezra, and June. June had two daughters, Carlene and Rosey, from her failed marriage. The six girls, ages 6 to 13, had a marvelous time together.

Everyone in Nashville seemed to be pulling for June and Johnny to get married. They frequently performed together and often were seen sitting side by side in a church.

Having messed up his first marriage, Johnny was in no hurry this time. Then on a stage in London, Ontario, before 5,000 people, Johnny impulsively called, "Hey, June, will you marry me?" June blushed with embarrassment.

"Go on with the show," she urged.

The audience began shouting, "Say yes! Say yes!"

"OK," June finally consented. "I'll marry you."

Johnny kissed her and whispered, "I had to ask."

They were wed March 1, 1968, at a church in Franklin, KY. Merle Kilgore, one of Johnny's old music buddies, was best man. Except for Merle's ripping his pocket in getting the ring out for Johnny, the ceremony went smoothly. A nonalcoholic reception, attended by hundreds of guests, was held that night at Johnny's lakeside home. The next morning the newlyweds started their first day together with Bible study.

"I Want to Tell You . . . I'm a Christian"

For some time Johnny's main teacher had been June's father, Ezra Carter, who had been helping Jimmie Snow. Johnny spent hours and hours in his father-in-law's library. He couldn't learn enough about the Bible.

If the Bible said to make restitution for past wrongs, Johnny wanted to do it. And if the Bible said help the widows and orphans, he wanted to do that, too. Johnny Cash always had been known for his generosity. Now his interest in helping others was increased tenfold. Not surprisingly, as word got around about the new Johnny Cash, he was besieged by preachers and representatives of Christian causes.

He and June went to Israel as a follow-up to their Bible studies. Just after their return, old friend Luther Perkins died from burns he suffered from a fire in his home. Saying goodbye to such a good friend was very tough for Johnny.

Then their good friend, Jan Howard, lost a son in Vietnam. During and after the funeral they spent a lot of time with Jan. When a promoter spoke to them about a tour of American bases in the war zone, they agreed to go. The trip exhausted Johnny; in Vietnam he caught a terrible cold. He asked a doctor for pills and also drank some alcohol, the first time since the experience in the Georgia jail. His skin crawled; muscle spasms racked him. Feeling groggy he stumbled around in a daze. Both he and June knew he had slipped.

Waiting at the Saigon airport to board a plane for a show in Tokyo they met Jimmie Snow, who'd arrived to sing and preach for the troops. Johnny knew his condition was not hidden from the preacher who once had been on drugs himself. As they exchanged a few words, Jimmie looked him straight in the eye but said nothing about the obvious.

The Tokyo concert was a humiliating experience. Barely able to stand on stage, Johnny staggered through the performance. He closed by apologizing for being in such bad shape and vowed that no audience ever would see him that way again. After he and June prayed in their hotel, he flushed his remaining pills down the commode. They flew home.

During 1969 Columbia Records sold six million Johnny Cash records, one of every five Country records marketed in the United States that year. The Opry took him back. ABC-TV signed him for a series of shows. He set up his own company, the House of Cash, to publish music and to market Johnny Cash products. He and June had a son, John Carter Cash.

The television series received good ratings, but Johnny

wasn't pleased with some of the guests brought on by the producers. He also was unhappy about pressure to keep quiet about his Christian convictions. When the time arrived for the closing hymn on the next show, Johnny said, "I've sung lots of hymns and gospel songs, but this time I want to tell you that I feel what I'm about to sing. I'm a Christian." Soon afterward he heard that the network was unhappy and intended to drop his show.

During tapings Jimmie Snow dropped by to say hello. Keeping silent about Johnny's relapse in Vietnam, he invited Johnny to "come and knock off a few songs at church in memory of Luther [Perkins]." The Cashes still were going to a round of churches. Johnny and June honored Jimmie's request but didn't immediately commit themselves to Evangel Temple, the church in which so many of their friends were involved.

"I Love You, Little Sister . . . "

Johnny's sister Reba had helped him set up the family company, the House of Cash. His sister Joanne arrived from Houston and began working for the company. "I was just divorced and was drinking and on drugs," she recalls, "and if it hadn't been for my children, I might have committed suicide. In this condition I called Johnny. He told me to come to Nashville.

"'I love you, little sister, and want you,' he told me. I threw my three kids in the car and drove straight through—so stoned with drugs that afterward I couldn't remember the trip."

Dottie Lee, daughter of old-time Country performers Radio Dot and Smokey, then was the receptionist at the House of Cash. She recently had become a Christian at Evangel Temple.

Day after day Dottie kept reminding Joanna that Christ could solve her problems. Joanne finally told her, "Dottie, please forget about me. There's no hope. I'm too far gone."

Every October the Cash family held a reunion in Arkansas. Johnny rented a plane for flying his family and sisters over. On the way back they flew into a fierce thunderstorm. As the plane bounced in the black air, Johnny saw that Joanne was white with fright. He made the OK sign with his thumb and finger, but Joanne began screaming, "Jesus, help me! Jesus, help me! Jesus, if You'll save us, I'll go to church with Dottie." Joanne was sure this was her last chance.

The next Sunday as Joanne was entering Evangel Temple, a powerful force seemed to knock her back. She ran, jumped into her car, and drove home,

All that week she felt miserable. Sunday morning she went back and sat in the second row. When Jimmie Snow gave the invitation for salvation, she was first at the altar. She prayed for two hours "not for Jesus to save me," she says, "but for me to accept that He really did love me." Joanne later married Harry Yates, a minister in the church. They served together in an evangelistic ministry.

Celebrities at Church

Late one afternoon Johnny called Jimmie Snow: "Would you like to see my little place of worship?" he asked. Jimmie went over; they jumped into Johnny's Jeep and drove to a little cabin in the woods. By the time they arrived dark had fallen. "Would you dedicate my little church to the Lord?" Johnny asked.

Jimmie prayed; then Johnny asked God for strength and guidance. They talked for a half-hour before they returned to Johnny's house. Jimmie urged Johnny to get his whole family in one church where they could have regular Christian fellowship and hear the Word of God.

A couple of weeks later the whole Cash family went to Evangel Temple. Johnny saw his sister Joanne in the choir. She was smiling. The congregation sang *At the Cross* and *Standing on the Promises*, familiar, old-time songs which Johnny remembered from his childhood in Arkansas. Larry Gatlin then sang *Help Me*—Johnny thought it was the best song he had ever heard

The Cashes returned the next Sunday and heard Jimmie emphasize that a father should be the spiritual leader of his household. Johnny talked down to the altar. "Jimmie," he said, "if my house is going to serve the Lord, I need to lead the way." June and the children followed.

Evangel Temple, already known as the "Church of the Country-Music Stars", became an even greater attraction with Johnny and June Cash. On any Sunday people might hear Connie Smith, Johnny Cash, Billy Walker, Larry Gatlin, and Kris Kristofferson. Kris also had gone to the altar at Evangel Temple and had written a couple of gospel songs afterward. *Why Me, Lord?* is the gospel classic he wrote after he heard Jimmie Snow preach on God's unconditional love.

Trying to protect the celebrities and keep the services worshipful, church elders posted a sign requesting that visitors neither solicit autographs nor take pictures inside the building. The church also had to turn down requests from persons wanting to sing in front of the congregation, because so many wanted to pitch their music to the stars.

Keeping people away from Johnny Cash became impossible. He and June were there every time the doors opened. They often went to the altar to pray with penitents. One Sunday a man seated near Johnny followed him to the altar. They were hardly on their knees when the "seeker" whipped out a sheet of music and whispered loudly, "Hey, Johnny, listen to this song I've written. I just know it will be a hit."

Johnny was used to this sort of boldness, but at the altar of his church? "Brother," he said kindly, "this isn't the place. Go to my office tomorrow. My secretary will give you an appointment." He later listened to the writer, but the song didn't catch his fancy.

After they joined Evangel Temple, Johnny and June made another visit to Israel. Johnny was gripped with the desire to make a film about Jesus—one which would be true to Scripture and down-to-earth so that ordinary people could understand why Jesus was sent to earth and what He could do for them today. He asked Jimmie Snow to be his consultant. In 1971 they took about 30 people to the Holy Land for the production. Larry Gatlin sang *Help Me* and another song called *Last Supper* which was written just for the film. Kris Kristofferson sang *Burden of Freedom*, a new song he had written.

More than a year was required to get the movie, "The Gospel Road", ready for theaters. Johnny appeared personally at film premiers in major cities. His old pastor friend, Floyd Gressett, now retired from the ministry, took the film to every prison that would give him permission to show it. No accurate tally of decisions for Christ was made, but the professions of faith certainly numbered in the thousands. One missionary reported 50,000 "commitments to Christ" that resulted from film showings in Africa alone.

The "Statesman" of Country Music

Ezra Carter, Johnny's Bible mentor, was now dead. Johnny and June inherited Ezra's large library of biblical and historical works. They enrolled in Bible correspondence courses and faithfully kept up their lessons at home and on tour. Drawn to the plight of orphans they built two orphanages near their vacation home in Jamaica. Johnny also served as president of the Autistic Foundation for Children in the United States.

When during the International Year of the Child he was recognized for his concern for children, Johnny said, "We are our brother's keeper. The whole future of the human race may depend on whether we reach out a helping hand to the homeless and the poor."

For all of his good works and reputation for helping people Johnny Cash was not immune from slanderous stories in the media.

Johnny told reporter-friends, "I swear I've never used heroin or sniffed cocaine. I'm not on pills and haven't been since I was cured several years ago. And June and I are too much in love to ever think of being separated."

Johnny said he had to cancel appearances with Billy Graham because Johnny had fallen and hurt his leg. "It's a good thing I'm a Christian," he declared. "If I wasn't, I'd break the jaws of three or four people in this town for getting those stories out."

Johnny Cash continues to be highly regarded and trusted in the Country-music community. When a tragedy hits a family, he often is called on to speak at a memorial service.

On March 16, 1991 seven members of Reba McEntire's band, along with her tour manager and two pilots, were killed when their private plane crashed in a mountainous area in Southern California. They were en route to a tour date in Indiana. A second plane, carrying other members of the group, arrived safely.

Later in the week a memorial service was held at Christ Church in Brentwood, TN. Reba called Johnny and asked him to speak.

Accompanying himself on an acoustic guitar, Johnny sang *Jim, I Wore a Tie Today*, written by Cindy Walker. When time arrived to say the name in the song, Johnny replaced it with the name of each of the deceased. Repeating the names he added, "I wore it for you." He ended the song with the request, "When you get to the streets of gold, stake a claim for me."

Johnny noted that his own mother had been buried a week before Reba called him. He told of telling Willie Nelson how he had performed on stage two days after his mother's death. Johnny said Willie told him, "It is our way of life."

Johnny Cash continues to be as popular as ever with Country fans. He can't possibly fulfill all the requests for performances. At times 30 to 40 fan buses line the road leading to his lakeside home. Security guards are posted to keep people from climbing the fence surrounding the house.

In 1991, not long after he spoke at the memorial for Reba McEntire's friends in Brentwood, a development company announced plans for a $35 million Cash Country theme park and museum on a 65-acre plot in Branson, MO. Johnny said he and June probably would live part of the year in Branson.

In April 1992 reports emerged stating that work had been stopped on the project when the contractors went unpaid. A later story said the developer had filed for bankruptcy reorganization. Johnny Cash, who was to have performed at the theater, is said to have no financial interest in the property.

Whether or not he moves to Branson, Johnny Cash has no intention of retiring. Expect him at 80, with silver hair and a face deeply etched with lines and scars, to still be greeting audiences with, "Hello, I'm Johnny Cash." And the purposeful stride and familiar, husky quaver always will be distinctively that of "The Man in Black" who has become the statesman of Country music.

Chapter 8
Country Comics

A Country-music show would really be missing something without Roy Acuff "walking the dog" with his yo-yo on the stage or balancing a fiddle bow in the end of his nose, while the crowd *ooohs* in admiration.

Nor without Cousin Minnie Pearl, the "Belle of Grinder's Switch", waltzing across stage swirling her green organdy skirt with the familiar pricetag swinging from her $1.98 flower-and-vegetable-topped hat. Coquettishly tossing her head and shrieking, "Howdeeee, I'm jist so proud to be hyar", she rolls into her humorous lines:

"You know sumpin'? I had my pitcher tuk. I shore did. I said to the photographer, 'That pitcher doesn't do me justice.'

"'Lady,' he said, 'you don't need justice. You need mercy.'

"I'd like to shake hands with all the ladies and kiss all the fellers. I kin get the hand-shakin over in a hurry, but the kissin' take timmmmmmmme. I ain't been kissed in so long that I fergit whether you should draw in yer breath er blow it out."

Nor without Jerry Clower swooping across the stage at the Opry in Nashville or the Grand Palace Theater in Branson in ruffled yellow shirt and tux, a glittering Star of David swinging from a gold chain around his neck: "Whooooie, I shore feel good tonight. Whooooie! I'm gonna tell ya 'bout me and ma brother, Sonny, killin' rats. We wuz up in the corn crib and Sonny caught the hugest rat I ever did see. It was such a fine rat, he run into the house to show it to Mama.

"Now Sonny didn't know that Reverend Brock, the Baptist preacher, was there visitin' Mama. Sonny done rushed into the living room and said, 'Looka hyar, Mama, at what a rat I got. I done whupped 'em over the head with an ear of corn; I done stomped him three or four times.'

"Then Sonny up and saw that preacher. Oh, I'll tell ya, his eyes got bigggg. He hugged that ole dead rat up to his chest and stroked hit and cried. And he said, 'And preacher, the good Lord done called the poor thang home.'"

Then there's the cornspun humor of Hee-Haw,

"Hey, Grandpa! Whut's for supper?" yells the chorus and Grandpa Jones recites:

Vinegar-season collard greens,
A heapin' pot of pinto beans,
Hot buttered cornbread piled in a stack,
And a slice of onion that'll bite ya back.

Country Corn

And the corn grinds on. What would Country-music shows be without the comics?

The funnies of Minnie Pearl, Jerry Clower, Grandpa Jones, and other side-splitters are straight out of the rural America from which so many musicians have sprung. The stories heard on the Opry, Hee-Haw, in theaters along the Branson Strip, and on other stages have been told around countless campfires and house-raisings, at innumerable pie suppers and quilting bees, and in circles of whittlers killing time around pot-bellied stoves in general stores when the weather was too dry for planting or too wet for plowing.

Whether in song, skit, or monologue, old-time Country humor was about everyday life which the people understood. Many stories involved preachers, churches, angels, and Bible characters. Country-music fans today are still hearing:

Two old maids were comin' out of church.
"Doris," one says to the other, "There shore wasn't as many in sarvice today."
"No, there warn't. When the preacher said, 'dearly beloved', I thought he was proposin' to one of us."

The other night I was in a church what the preacher passed the hat after his sermon. It took a long time, but finally the hat come back with nary a penny. The preacher shook it, turned it upside down, and said, "Thankee, Lord, that I got back my hat from these skinflints."

Tom Hatfield's little girl asked him, "Pa, why don't angels have whiskers?"
"Wal, I reckon hit's 'cause they got to heaven by a close shave."

Corny to some folks perhaps, but such humor makes "Country" bellies bounce.

Old-Time Fun-Makers

The names of the old-time musical groups and the tunes they sang were enough to elicit smiles. How could an audience keep from grinning when the Skillet Lickers took off on *Flop-eared Mule, Sally, Let Me Chaw Yer Rosin Some* and *You Can't*

Make a Monkey Out of Me. When Uncle Dave Macon, the Dixie Dewdrop, for example, thumbed his banjo to *Rabbit in the Pea Patch, Carve that 'Possom,* or *The Cross-eyed Butcher and the Cackin' Hen,* the crowds chuckled.

The old-time entertainers played all the strings of human emotion—from heartbreakers to rib-ticklers. One minute a performer would be wailing about "dear old Mother lying . . . in a lonely graveyard . . . 'neath the cold, cold clay." The next time he would be bouncing with *The Old Hen Cackled and the Rooster's Gonna Crow,* a rather earthy ditty about fowl sex.

Many old-time songs had humorous lines. For example, Alfred Reed's ballad, *How Can a Poor Man Stand Such Times and Live?* included a line about "preachers who preach for dough and not for soul; that's what keeps a poor man in a hole."

Roy Acuff: A Good-Humor Man

Many of the older Country comics and musicians as well rode on the tailgates of medicine wagons. Roy Acuff, Jimmie Rodgers, Gene Autry, and Bob Wills are only four who made their first show tours with the peddlers of patent medicines.

Roy Acuff might not be the King of Country Music today had he not traveled a summer with Dr. Hauer's medicine show out of Knoxville, TN. At the time young Roy was recovering from a sunstroke, which had dashed his hopes of a professional baseball career.

Dr. Hauer lived down the street from the Acuffs. He liked Roy's fiddling and easy banter and offered him a dollar a day to fiddle, sing, and tell jokes. Roy's preacher-father said, "I always wanted to travel with a medicine show myself, son. Go ahead and enjoy yourself."

In the summer of 1932 Roy, Doc Hauer, and veteran musician Jake Tindell left Knoxville in Doc's Reo sedan. They played mountain towns across East Tennessee and Virginia. They performed and peddled patent remedies in county-seat public squares.

When a crowd gathered, Roy struck up a fast fiddle time with Jake accompanying on his guitar. Between numbers they told Hee-Haw type jokes and did skits, which Roy later would use on the Opry. Sometimes Roy played a minstrel role. Other times he'd mimic an overgrown hillbilly boy, a young girl, or an old mountaineer.

Between acts and after the show, Doc gave his pitches: "Step right up, folks. Only one dollar for a bottle of Mocoton Tonic. Guaranteed to cure worms, dyspepsia, sick headaches, constipation, indigestion, pain in the side, back and limbs, and a torpid liver."

Doc also sold soaps, candy, and a sure cure for corns on toes. To demonstrate he would pour the stuff over a volunteer's work shoes. The brew would seep through the leather and numb the man's feet. It would make hin believe his corns had been dissolved.

From the 1930s on, every Country-music show on the radio carried a comedian. The most famous early comics outside the Opry were Lulu Belle and Scotty (Myrtle Cooper and Scott Wiseman), who kept WLS, Chicago audiences happy for more than 20 years. Married both on the stage and in real life, Lulu Belle played a brash, pushy, fussy wife who picked fights and kept the cheerful Scotty in line.

Every old-time musician had a repertoire of stories and stunts. Roy Acuff developed his fiddle-bow act by balancing cornstalks when he was a boy. Eventually he was able to raise a plow in the air, balance it on his chin, and walk around the field with it. His father saw him one day and warned, "Son, you're goin to kill yourself if you don't stop that."

Decades later, when President Richard Nixon visited for the opening show in the new Opry House, he pulled a yellow yo-yo from his coat. Dangling it at the end of the string in a futile attempt to imitate Roy, he said, "I haven't learned to use this thing yet." When Roy tried to teach him the art of yo-yoing, the President interrupted: "Roy, I'll stay here and learn to yo-yo. You go to Washington and be President."

"Bashful" Brother Oswald

Until his illness a familiar sight in floppy hat, overalls, and work shoes on the Opry was 80-year-old "Bashful" Brother Oswald (Pete Kirby) imitating Roy's yo-yo with one the size of a tricycle tire. Os, who raised hysterics by clomping with the girl cloggers on the Opry stage, is one of Roy's longest associations.

Os learned to play the guitar and banjo when he was a boy in his native Smoky Mountains. He also sold moonshine whiskey for his father. After an unsuccessful try at Country music in Chicago, Os returned home and joined Roy Acuff's "Crazy Tennesseans", known today as the "Smokey Mountain Boys."

When Roy brought on Rachel Veach, an 18-year-old banjo player, they began to get letters asking how she could remain a lady and travel with a bunch of men. One day while they were riding in the car, Os gave his trademark horse laugh. Roy thought he sounded like a bashful boy and said, "I'm gonna make you Rachel's brother and put you two on as 'Rachel and her great big, bashful brother, Oswald.'" So he did; that stopped the critical mail.

Os and Rachel each had a blackened tooth. Os wore a black wig, checked visor cap, and big britches with suspenders. Rachel wore long bloomers, which kept dropping below her dress, and high-buttoned shoes with white stockings. They laughed, told jokes, sang funny songs, and convulsed crowds.

Oswald drank heavily until 1969, when doctors warned that he would die from liver disease if he didn't stop. He never touched a drop after that but continued to use a half-pint whiskey bottle of water for his act. He'd bring on an explosive device called the "smudge pot". It was loaded with smoke bombs, black gunpowder, and firecrackers.

When Os took a swig from the bottle, Roy complained about drinking on stage. Os then spat out the water in a long arc at the smudge pot. Touched off by an offstage band member, the incendiaries exploded in a blanket of black smoke.

More Opry Comedians

Besides Roy and Os and Rachel, the Opry has had a whole string of comedians: Uncle Dave Macon, Lonzo and Oscar, Cousin Jody, the Duke of Paducah, Jamup and Honey, Rod Brasfield, Stringbean Ackerman, and numerous others.

Uncle Dave mainly was a banjo picker, but he could be funny. An old handbill announced:

LOOK WHO'S COMING
UNCLE DAVE MACON & SAM MCGEE
FROM TENNESSEE
FUNNY CLEAN JOKES AND LOTS OF FUN
BRING THE WHOLE FAMILY

Some of the funniest stories were told on Uncle Dave. One originated in a recording studio where they had trouble with his foot-stomping. Someone finally put a pillow under the foot. "Take it away," he ordered. "If I cain't hear my foot, I cain't hold the rhythm."

Lonzo and Oscar started singing and poking fun at each other and at others on the Opry during World War II. Two of their biggest hits were *I'm My Own Grandpa* and *Did You Have to Bring that Up While I Was Eating?* The original Oscar still performs, but the act has a third Lonzo (the first withdrew; the second died of a heart attack.)

Cousin Jody, a talent on the Dobro (resonated) guitar, started with Roy Acuff. With floppy hat, checkered suspenders, and Purina feed-sack pants he was a sight when he made his chin touch his nose.

Black-faced Jamup and Honey, whom I loved when I was a boy, were portrayed by Bunny Biggs and Honey Wild, who also played some side-splitting side characters: Joe Blow, Firecracker, One Flung, Tuff Stuff Huffman, Pancho, and many others. In days when minstrel acts were acceptable, they were a riot on the Opry.

Rod Bradfield, who flirted with Minnie Pearl on stage, died in 1958. Said the pastor at his funeral: "I expect to see Rod just inside the golden gates and hear him say as he so often asked on the Opry, 'Come on in, Preacher. Where in the cat hair have your been?'"

Stringbean Ackerman, one of the most beloved Country comics, grew up as Dave Ackerman on a Kentucky farm and cared for little but banjo-picking, baseball, hunting, and fishing. He arrived on the Opry stage in 1942 with Bill and Charlie Monroe. A fiddler named him "Stringbean."

On the Opry and later on Hee-Haw, Stringbean wore a low-waisted suit. With his sadsack delivery, knees knocking, and eyes flipping up and down like they were window shades, lovable Stringbean could bring down the house.

The "Stringbean" Murders

Stringbean and "Mrs. String", as his wife, Estelle, was called, lived in a little three-room red house near Grandpa and Ramona Jones outside Nashville.

Stringbean's favorite hobby was fishing. He and Grandpa spent many hours together on the lake with neither saying a word. Stringbean owned 20 Cadillacs but never drove one. "My wife don't tell me how to fish and I don't tell her how to drive," he often said. He joked about Estelle as "the only woman I know that can swealler a banana sideways", but he clearly loved her deeply. One seldom was seen without the other.

Both were known to carry large amounts of money in their clothing. At 10:20 p.m. on Saturday, November 10, 1974, Stringbean played his banjo and sang, *I'm Going to the Grand Ole Opry* and *Make Myself a Name*. It was to be his last time on stage.

The next morning Grandpa Jones arrived to take Stringbean on a hunting trip to Virginia and found both Ackermans dead from gunshot wounds. The robbers had waited for them to arrive home from the Opry and attacked them as they were entering the house. The criminals missed $3,300 hidden in a secret pocket on Stringbean's bib overalls and another $2,200 tucked in a tobacco sack pinned inside Estelle's clothing. Later they were caught and sentenced to long prison terms. One claimed he had been drinking and smoking marijuana and could not recall what happened.

At the funeral, flower arrangements in the shape of a fish and a steering wheel adorned the caskets. Two hearses rolled side by side at the head of a long funeral procession. "One of the prettiest sights I've ever seen, in spite of the sadness," Roy Acuff said.

"Stringbean," murmured a mournful Grandpa Jones, "wouldn't have hurt a fly."

How "Grandpa" Got His Name

"Grandpa" Louis Jones, the "old" fellow with the floppy hat, bushy moustache, baggy pants, suspenders, and rubber boots, was also born in Kentucky. The youngest of 10 children in a tenant farm family, he says, "We moved so much that every time the wagon backed up to the door, the chickens laid down and crossed their legs."

As a boy Louis learned to play a guitar brought to work by an employee at a sawmill. When the mill closed, one of his brothers bought him a steel guitar for 75 cents at a junk shop. At 16 he won $50 in a talent contest and was on his way to musical fame.

"My mother told me to get into a good, solid profession— something that would pay me well and last," Louis says. "I never did like working, so I went into music and comedy."

At age 22 he got the name *Grandpa* when he performed with Bradley Kincaid over a Boston radio station: "Get up here to the microphone. You're just like an ole Grandpa," Kincaid reportedly said.

Grandpa recalls, "I was tired from performing every night and people said I sounded like 80. So I fixed myself up with a false moustache. I was the awfulest sight you ever saw. Now I don't need much to make me look the part." In 1992 Grandpa was 77.

After he took the name, Grandpa Jones performed on a string of stations. In 1946, the year Grandpa joined the Opry, he met his match in Ramona Riggins, a coal-miner's daughter, who played four instruments and sang harmony. Soon after, they got married and continued to work together.

In 1969 Grandpa joined Hee-Haw and considers the show "one of the greatest things that ever happened to me. I reckon people like to see somebody make a fool of himself."

Grandpa "loves to see people laugh, especially children. That's when I think I'm doing a little something worthwhile in this old world . . . In the old days nearly every show had a slapstick comedian. Most of 'em had a ring around one toe and were called Elmer . . . I keep trying things 'til I find something that works. If the audience is cold, I may pick out one person and play to him. If I can get just one laughing, it can spread to the whole audience."

For a while Grandpa performed with the old radio team, Lum and Abner, and still uses some of their jokes. He also tells stories about relatives and on himself. "I had an uncle who was so bald he had to draw a chalk mark up to here to tell where to wash his face." He freely admits that sometimes he's absent-minded. Once he spent an entire day looking over his farm for a cow and then remembered that the animal was in his freezer waiting to be cooker.

He thinks the old-time music is the best. "Some people call me old and dyed-in-the-wool, but I really believe the older style is returning. A lot of today's Country music can't be told from pop."

Without question Hee-Haw has had the most comedians of any Country show. One of the best, before his death in a plane crash, was the late Reverend Grady Nutt. Billed as the "Prime Minister of Humor", Nutt—his real name—was a seminary-trained preacher with experience as a Southern Baptist pastor before he turned full-time humorist: "I was pastor of a rural church where the parking-lot potholes were so deep, you could be baptized in them."

Lulu's Story

Of all the singers and comics who have performed on Hee-Haw, none has a more dramatic and pathetic story than LuLu Roman, the big girl who draws laughs by simply rolling her eyes. LuLu's pilgrimage from drugs and wild living to a new life in Christ is related in her biography published by Fleming H. Revell and simply titled *LuLu*.

Born Bertha Louise Hable, LuLu never knew her father. Shortly after LuLu's birth her parents divorced. Even the relationship with her mother was distant. When LuLu was 4, her grandmother put her in a Baptist orphans home in Texas.

She kept expecting her grandmother to return for her. "She isn't coming," a housemother said sternly. "You're going to live with us now." When LuLu began sobbing, the woman warned, "If you make another sound, I'll blister you." That night LuLu wet the bed and got a severe spanking.

The home operated by rigid rules: everything—getting up, washing, dressing, eating, marching to school, and sleeping—was programmed by whistles and bells. The housemothers kept close tabs on every resident. The housemothers kept close tabs on every resident. The children had to eat everything on their plates. LuLu's only private place was her tiny closet.

LuLu always seemed to be in trouble. Once when she looked up at a housemother, the insensitive woman shouted at her, "Don't you buck those eyes at me!"

Visitors could arrive for only one hour on Saturday. On Sunday church attendance was mandatory—two hours in the morning and two in the evening. The preachers pounded their Bibles and shook their fingers at the children. At night LuLu lay awake terrified at the thought of dying.

She was allowed to take piano lessons. One day a house-mother found her playing "Chopsticks" on the piano with her bare toes. The housemother didn't realize LuLu was only try- ing to get attention from the girls laughing around her. "No more lessons!" the woman screamed.

When LuLu began helping in the kitchen, she resolved her frustrations by eating. She also loved plays and putting on funny faces at Halloween. She could disguise her face but not the pudgy body of which she as so ashamed.

When LuLu reached the 10th grade, the girls were bussed outside to a high school, where they were teased about being from the home. LuLu learned to smoke. She also began sneak- ing out at night and became acquainted with drugs.

On high-school graduation, LuLu received $50, a set of luggage, an outfit of clothing, and a list of job prospects. She and a girlfriend got an apartment and became more heavily involved in drugs. They both were hired as telephone opera- tors, but LuLu became sarcastic with callers. After she swore at a man making a long-distance call, the phone company fired her.

She moved in with a couple of ex-residents of the orphans home who reportedly were selling drugs, forging checks, and buying merchandise on stolen credit cards. LuLu was caught trying to use a stolen card and put on probation.

Penniless, she roomed with a go-go dancer and got work in a nightclub. Wearing huge clown bloomers, a red bow in her hair, and another on her back, she bounced on stage, rolled her eyes, and licked a big sucker. The customers went wild.

She bought a new Continental car and fell in love with a man named Harry, who soon moved in with her. One night she returned home early and found him in her bed with another girl. When she chased them out, Harry took LuLu's new car and left.

"Dear God, get me out of this mess," she prayed. She had- n't prayed since she was in the sixth grade.

Then Buck Owens' manager called her unexpectedly. "We're putting together a cornball answer to 'Laugh In.' We want you to be 'Goldie Hawn.'" LuLu wore a pink dress with ruffles and big buttons and was a sensation on television.

Later moving to Nashville for tapings on the new Hee-Haw, she spent money wildly. She bought another Continental and furnished a new home with psychedelic posters and astrological charts. Harry returned. He begged forgiveness and moved back in.

"I was trying to fill up that hole inside me," LuLu says. "I was foul-mouthed and arrogant and obnoxious."

When Harry discovered that LuLu was pregnant, he left again. Police caught her with five-and-a-half pounds of marijuana. She was dropped from the Hee-Haw show. A lawyer got the marijuana-possession charge dismissed; she moved to Dallas.

Desperate and seeing no reason for living, LuLu took an overdose of pills, turned up her stereo, and lay down to die. A friend stopped by just in time. When LuLu's baby was born, the doctor told her the infant boy wouldn't make it through the night. LuLu cried out to God. The baby survived, but LuLu went back to selling drugs.

Diane, the younger sister of a friend from the orphans home, stopped by to see her, "I want to help you, LuLu," she said. "I love you. Jesus wants to help you. He loves you."

For several months, while LuLu was out of work, Diane and another friend cared for LuLu and the baby, paid the rent, and bought groceries. LuLu reluctantly went with then to the Beverly Hills Baptist Church in Dallas.

She agreed to talk with the pastor. "I was so bad," LuLu recalls, "I would say things such as, 'I might become a Christian, but I won't stop smoking marijuana.' He'd come back with, 'Well, God can take care of that.'"

"I was into 'Let's freak the preacher out.' I was really bad, but he kept returning with an answer for everything I said. He loved me through all of it."

Seeing through LuLu's facade, the pastor asked, "Will you go on carrying this load, or will you lay it at the foot of the cross?" They knelt together while LuLu said a simple sinner's prayer. She got up feeling lighter; all the way home she kept shouting, "Praise the Lord!"

During the next few months she basically went nowhere except to church. Christian friends helped her care for the baby. Then a church asked her to give her testimony. One invitation led to another. Soon she was speaking to churches and youth crusades and making television appearances across the country.

At the Hee-Haw offices she told her old friends about the change in her life. Before she left, the management asked her to return to the show.

In years after that she made special appearances on several network programs. She married a Christian man, Woody Smith. She and Woody and their two teen-aged sons now live in Dallas. "We tell our boys," LuLu says, "'Love the Lord with all your heart, acknowledging Him in all that you do, and He will acknowledge you. He will let you have your dreams.'"

"Howdee! This Hyar's Minnie Pearl"

The one and only Minnie Pearl—"Aunt Minnie" to the girls on Hee-Haw—has been a regular on the comedy show for many years. She entertained Opry audiences almost every Friday and Saturday night before she had a stroke. Her background is almost the opposite of LuLu's.

Born Sarah Ophelia Colley, the youngest of five sisters, she was reared in a loving, church-going family in the small town of Centerville, TN, about 50 miles southwest of Nashville. At age 3 Sarah appeared in her first recital, but she gave her most memorable performance two years later when she and a little cousin were to carry their aunt's bridal train in a society wedding. All went fine at the dress rehearsal. The next evening as the bride was moving toward the altar to the tune of *The Wedding March,* little Sarah suddenly dropped her end of the train, sat down on the floor, and began crying loudly. The wedding was thrown into confusion. Mrs. Colley rushed to her child's side. "What's wrong, honey? Tell Mother."

"Oh, Mama," Sarah wailed. "I'm not gonna do this again. Auntie was married last night."

Sarah survived the wedding and went on to become popular in high school. She made good grades, was a cheerleader, an expert tennis player, and always had plenty of dates.

Her parents sent her to Ward-Belmont College, a prestigious Baptist girls' school. Graduating in dramatics during the Depression, she returned home to Centerville to teach high school.

She quit teaching school to travel the Southeast and helped an Atlanta firm produce amateur shows for civic clubs. She met "Minnie Pearl" in an Appalachian mountain town and was captivated. "This woman treated me so beautifully and was so funny and told the wildest tales that I came away talking like her."

Later Sarah stopped at a resort hotel in South Carolina and was asked to help with a benefit show by dressing up in an old gingham dress and doing a routine. She bought a bright yellow dress for $1.98, a pair of flat-heeled slippers, white stockings, and a flat straw hat decked with fruits and flowers.

"Howdee," she called to the well-dressed crowd at the benefit. "I'm just so glad to be here. This hyar's Minnie Pearl.

Thyat's my name, Minnie Pearl, it is." The dignified guests laughed themselves silly.

Sarah returned to Centerville to help support her mother after her father died. Taking a job with the WPA she managed a recreation program for children. The future in dramatics for Sarah and Minnie Pearl seemed bleak. At 28 she believed she was a failure.

About a year later, in 1939, the Tennessee Banking Association in Centerville invited her to do her "Minnie Pearl" act. She impressed Nashville banker Bob Turner, who recommended her to the Opry. WSM gave her an audition but feared the resentment of some people who might believe she was putting them down. Nevertheless WSM agreed to let her perform at 11:05 p.m. Saturday when most of the Opry crowd would be gone and little harm would be done if she flopped. Her initial performance, for which she received $10, brought in more than 250 fan letters and led to a bid to join the Opry as a permanent member.

After more than 50 years of performing, Sarah remains unpretentious. "Minnie Pearl," she says, "is jist a lil' ole country gal who comes to town to flirt with the fellers but nothing serious, or she'd run all the way back to the farm."

"Minnie" sticks to the old jokes which audiences never seem to outgrow:

"I know this ole boy back home in Grinder's Switch. When he's told you 'Howdy', he's told you all he knows."
"Feller said to me the other day, 'Minnie, you look jist like a breath of spring.' Wal, he didn't quite say that. What he said was, 'You look like the end of a long, hard winter.'"
"Brother went into a blacksmith shop the other day and

137

picked up a hot horseshoe and dropped it right off.
'Burned ya, didn't it?' the blacksmith said.
"'Nope,' Brother told 'em. 'It jist don't take me long to
look at a horseshoe.'"
"And there's my Uncle Nabob. He's no failure. He jist
started at the bottom and liked it there.'"

Sarah has long been married to lawyer Henry Cannon.
Cannon manages her business matters and is an expert pilot
who used to fly her to show dates. He often accompanies her
to the Opry. One night I saw him there, standing in the stage
wing beaming, admiration glowing in his eyes, as Minnie
swept across the stage.

The Cannons have a beautiful Brentwood home in with a
swimming pool and tennis courts. They are involved in the
Nashville community and in the Methodist church. Sarah frequently has been asked to lend her name to worthy causes. She
has served, for example, as honorary chair of the Tennessee
Cancer Crusade and as chair of Heart Sunday in Tennessee.

For her 50th anniversary as a member of the Opry Sarah
was honored with an hour-long TV show on the TNN
Network. Friends such as Roy Acuff, Little Jimmy Dickens,
Connie Smith, Chet Atkins, and others performed and offered
their congratulations. Fifty-dozen roses arrived from fellow
performer Dwight Yoakam. These bouquets turned the Opry
stage into a bed of beauty.

Sarah Ophelia Cannon gives God the credit for directing
her life: "I always wanted to be an actress, but the Lord never
intended for me to go in that direction, because he knew I did-
n't have the talent. The Lord gave me Minnie Pearl and this
sense of humor to make people laugh and case a few burdens
in an aching world."

"The Mouth of the South"

If Minnie had a male counterpart in Country entertainment, it would have to be Jerry Clower, the whooping, howling, yarn-spinning ex-fertilizer salesman from Yazoo City, MS. One difference is that "this 275-pound canary—what is the heaviest act" in show business, according to Jerry, is the same person on and off stage, whether he's performing on the Opry, at the Grand Palace in Branson, or in some other great show-place.

Some will tell you that Jerry is the most respected Christian in Country entertainment. A Nashville preacher's wife, close to many Country performers, says, "Jerry's the only man I know who can come up and hug a woman on the street and cause no suspicion. He just naturally loves everybody and everybody knows he has one of the best marriages."

Interviewers will tell you that Jerry isn't bashful about talking about his wife or about anything else. His voice is almost loud enough to "bust" your tape recorder. So you stand back and tell him to fire away. He draws a crowd whether he's talking to a reporter backstage at the Opry, in Branson, or at the Southern Baptist Convention he attends almost every year. I once interviewed him when Southern Baptists met in Miami. All other activity in the press room eased as more than 100 editors and writers gathered around to hear "The Mouth of the South" as he often terms himself.

This was so when he was selling fertilizer in Mississippi for $17,000 a year. When he walked into a business and began to tell stories, the ears began flapping. Then he was invited to Nashville and the next year brought in $100,000 "for tellin' stories funny."

Jerry remembers the moment he first realized he had become a big-time entertainer: "I was a settin' in a hotel room

and readin" the *Nashville Banner* and there was a pitcher of
me and Tammy Wynette. They was a callin' both of us
'Country music stars.' I said to myself, 'A star? Why, I'm 44-
years old.' I phoned my wife in Yazoo City and said, 'Dahlin',
my soul, somethin's a happenin' to us. But I want you to know
that you're still the main-most woman in my life."

Jerry, who never forgets important dates, says that was the
year that his wife Homerline, then 44 herself, became pregnant
again: "After Ray, Amy, and Sue comin' so many years before,
we never figured on Katy. We had a lot more faith in that man
goin' to the moon than we did in Mama ever comin' up pregnant again. We thought our crop was laid by. Katy's the most
precious thing God ever did for us."

Jerry also remembers when he first saw Homerline. "It was
at a revival meeting, the Thursday night before the fourth
Sunday in July in 1939. We both publicly professed our faith
in Christ and were baptized in the East Fork of the Amity
River on Sunday. She was the most beautiful thing I'd ever
seen." She also was in the third grade. Jerry never looked
twice at another girl.

Jerry says "She's always been my number one. If God
gave me the ingredients to make a woman, I'd make her just
like Homerline. I praise God for her every day."

When he was a baby, Jerry's own parents were divorced.
He and his brother, Sonny, lived with their mother, who remarried when Jerry was 13. The brothers grew up milking cows,
rounding up calves, playing 'gator in the creek and Tarzan in
the trees, hunting coons and 'possums, going to school (Jerry
didn't miss a day in 12 years), and attending church twice on
Sunday and once in the middle of the week.

During World War II Jerry served in the Navy and earned
three battlestars. When he arrived home, he attended
Mississippi State University, where he became an outstanding

football lineman. He says, "The first college football game I ever saw was the one I played in."

With a degree in agriculture he served as an assistant county agent and then went to work for the Mississippi Chemical Company as a traveling fertilizer salesperson.

"You Can Make It without Being Vulgar"

After a few years he decided he was talking too much about fertilizer and not telling enough funny stories. That's when he started his famous coon-hunt yarn which friends insisted he record. "Jerry Clower from Yazoo City, Mississippi Talkin'" sold half a million and launched his showbiz career.

The coon story, which he still tells 200 times a year, is about the tree-top confrontation that occurred when professional tree-climber John Eubanks shinnied up the tallest sweet gum tree in Southern Mississippi to dislodge what he thought was a raccoon. It turned out to be a lynx, or, as Jerry says, "a souped-up wildcat." The story continues:

"'Waaaaaaooooooh! This thang's a killin me,' John yelled while the whole top of the tree was a shakin' and the dogs were bitin' the bark off the tree and a fightin' one another. 'Wooooie, shoot this thang.'

"The feller on the ground yelled back, 'John, I cain't shoot up thar. I might hit you.'

"'Wal, jist shoot up in hyar amongst us,' John screamed. One uf us has got to have some relief.'"

The coon story alone reportedly has made Jerry more than a million dollars.

On stage Jerry doesn't just talk when he tells a funny story. He bellows, wails, howls, screeches, contorts his face, furrows his brow, and puckers his lips. He also imitates a chainsaw, a diesel truck, and motorcycle, and a Brahmin bull.

He's never been known to tell an off-color joke. This helps explain why he's so popular. "It's a challenge to make people laugh with clean, non-risque humor," Jerry says. "I've proven that you can make it without being vulgar or obscene." Jerry also says he has no secret to his ability to "crack" an audience up: "It's the joy within whut comes from knowin' Jesus Christ."

Jerry has his "Christian convictions, but I try to be careful not to alienate myself from everyone. I don't want anyone in television to say, 'Let's don't get him back, for all he wants to do is preach.'"

Jerry can be riled, he admits, when he gets "a little irritated when I'm asked if I got religious after I became wealthy or before when it was less convenient. Most people what ask that kind of question has goatees."

Jerry also gets a little upset with people who say one can't live a Christian life and succeed as an entertainer.

"Look at me. I'm a G-rated comic performing in an X-rated world. I don't lie, cheat, swear, smoke, drink, or chew. There ain't no X-rated comic whut has sold as many albums as I have. I think I'm livin' proof that you can live by your convictions and get along good."

Jerry has been named "Country Comedian of the Year" two years in a row by *Billboard, Cash Box,* and *Record World.* But his biggest honor, he says, occurred when he was installed as a member of the Grand Ole Opry. The governor of Mississippi traveled to the Opry for the installation.

When not traveling Jerry is at home in his hometown of Yazoo City, MS, where he's a deacon and lay preacher at the First Baptist church. Homerline teaches a girls' Sunday-school class there. The rule in their home always has been automatic church attendance. "Nobody need ask," says Jerry. They also tithe Jerry's professional income. The tithe amounts to much more than Jerry was making a year before he put his coon story on record.

Jerry's Christian beliefs have changed his ideas about race relations. "I'm a redneck, but I'm an educated redneck. I was taught that you should never have your mind so made up that facts couldn't change it. The Lord pricked my conscience and I changed my mind. I'm a Southern liberal now when civil rights is concerned."

Above all, Jerry wants to be known "as a Christian entertainer who performed on and off the stage and folks didn't have to figure out what kind of a mood he was in to approach him. I'd like for people to say, 'Well, ole Jerry wherever you saw him, he was praising the Lord. And he was Jerry Clower—the Christian comic—24 hours a day.'"

And that—as Jerry Clower might say, "shore ain't a joke."

Chapter 9
Ministries and Miracles

Across the country and within Nashville's Country-music community the evangelical movement boomed in the 1970s and 19890s. The changes in the lives of such stars as Connie Smith, Billy Walker, Jeannie C. Riley, and others made hot copy for newspapers and fan magazines. Much of the publicity centered around Nashville's Evangel Temple, then the fastest-growing church in the Assemblies of God denomination.

The story that got the biggest press was not pleasant for the Christian stars to read. Paul Harvey put it crisply: "Ex-Country music entertainer and preacher Jimmie Snow and Carol are divorcing."

Snow Stories in Nashville

The divorce was reported across the U.S. and Canada and even overseas. Columnists in fan magazines ran wild with speculation. Jimmie and Carol both were from prominent Country-music families. Their parents were among the few performers in the Opry whose marriages had endured. The Evangel Temple pastor and his wife had been presented as the ideal couple. He preached and she played the organ and directed the choir. For six years they had traveled together in evangelism. They'd been to Vietnam twice and had performed for troops in battle zones.

Many couldn't believe they were breaking up.

Jimmie himself later admitted that he had been too busy with the church to realize that they were growing apart. For years he had been going one way as he preached and counseled people, many with marital problems, in the church office and helping Johnny Cash with the film "The Gospel Road." Carol had been leading another life with her friends.

In August 1971 Jimmie told the church that he and Carol were separated. Later in the month, hoping to shake up Carol, he filed for divorce. Carol cross-filed. Since Jimmie believed she should have custody of their two children, he elected to withdraw his suit.

The church was in an uproar. About 50 members promptly joined other congregations.

Assemblies of God officials told Jimmie he could continue as pastor. But if he should remarry, they said, he would seriously jeopardize his standing in the denomination.

Another 50 members left.

Jimmie told the performers who had not left, "I want you to stay, but you could be further embarrassed by further association with me." Johnny Cash said he would not be swayed. Later Johnny would leave because of crowd pressures.

The pastor's breakup made the ninth divorce in the church that year. In the previous six years only four Evangel Temple couples had parted ways.

The months after Jimmie's divorce were the most difficult in his Christian life. He often thought of quitting the ministry and returning to show business, the only other vocation he knew. Yet during his darkest night more conversions were registered than in any previous six-month time in the history of the church.

He and Carol agreed not to release any details of their divorce.

A year later Jimmie married Dottie Lee, the receptionist at the House of Cash. She had been converted at Evangel Temple; Jimmie and Dottie had known each other since they were children. Her parents, Radio Dot and Smokey, during the '40s and '50s had sung on the Opry. A beautiful blonde, Dottie already had been through two marriages and had four children.

Dottie was well-liked, but the new marriage stirred up the church even more. Another exodus took place. Denominational leaders asked Jimmie to turn in his ordination papers. Without them he no longer could be pastor of an Assemblies of God church. Evangel Temple solved this problem by withdrawing from the denomination. Jimmie continued as pastor. Dottie took Carol's place at the organ. But Jimmie's divorce and remarriage had sullied his influence and damaged the church's outreach.

Finding God at the Lord's Chapel

As Evangel Temple's star dimmed, a new church with a strong outreach to Country-music people was springing up in the Brentwood area. By 1980 it would become the largest non-Catholic congregation in Nashville and would involve many Country-music stars in the ministry.

Founder Billy Ray Moore, a veteran Assemblies of God pastor, was serving as pastor of First Assembly in Nashville, when the church was caught up in change. Blacks began attending, then long-haired hippies, then trendy, well-dressed professionals. Old-line Pentecostals were concerned that some of the women newcomers wore makeup and pantssuits. They saw the newcomers as a threat to the status quo. Pastor Moore disagreed and left to start a new work.

Thirty-three attended the first service in an old mansion in south Nashville. Within two months more than 200 were

attending. They named the new church "The Lord's Chapel", since, as Moore put it, "it doesn't belong to any person or denomination but to the Lord. Everyone is welcome."
Pastor Moore was determined to make the church visitor-friendly. He threw out the customary formal order of service. He stopped taking up a collection and told worshipers they could drop their gifts in an offering chest at the back. Instead of inviting people to walk to an altar at the front, he urged anyone with a need to go to a counseling room and pray with a counselor while the service was going on. And he encouraged the people to hold Bible studies and prayer meetings in their homes so neighbors and friends could attend. "Let's minister to people where we find them instead of trying to talk folks into coming to Sunday services," he said.

Thee new church outgrew the mansion and built an auditorium, which later burned. Members constructed a larger sanctuary to seat 1,500, but this proved to be too small. They bought more property and put up a still-larger building. With people attending from all over the Nashville area, they started four "daughter" churches in outlying areas.

Country-music people flocked to the services. Some, including Connie Smith and Donna Stoneman, became counselors.

Donna Stoneman: "Nothing has ever been so fulfilling as serving Jesus"

Country fans remember Donna Stoneman, the dancing, blonde, look-alike of actress of Debbie Reynolds, as "the world's best mandolin player." Her feet would move in synchronization with her fingers, as she plucked away on the mandolin. "Five-foot-two, eyes of blue, turned-down toes, turned-up nose," laughs Donna.

"That image started out being a part of me; then it got to be all of me and the real me got lost in the shuffle.

"I always had to keep smiling and dancing, while inside I was about to die. I hid it from the world. Everything became dark to me . . . I didn't understand why I was born, why I was living . . .. Just like all the young kids trying to find answers in drugs, I couldn't find any meaning in life.

"My husband and I weren't number-one rich, but we had enough. For somebody from a poor background, it was a lot, We had a big, beautiful house and I had four closets full of beautiful clothes. I had everything and yet I had nothing."

"My marriage failure was the last straw. I was estranged from my husband and lived for a year in a separate room in the same house. I stayed for the family's sake. for the business, for the sake of people. But every time I went smiling and dancing on stage, I could hardly keep from breaking down.

"For a year I contemplated how to kill myself. I didn't have access to pills—never was a pill-taker. I didn't have a gun, so I couldn't blow my brains out. The only thing I had was a razor blade. So I would sit on the floor with that blade and think how I might do it.

"I belonged to a cold, structured church. I had stopped going and they didn't even miss me. I was morally good. I made a vow when I was little that I would never drink alcohol, because I had lived around alcoholics and seen what it did. So I promised Jesus I wouldn't drink. But I had never asked HIm into my life. So I blamed Him for my troubles and He wasn't even my God.

"My friend, Cathy Manzer, came over. Cathy had been a nun. She just had a form of religion; later she got salvation. She said, 'Donna, pray.'

"I said, 'I'm not going to pray. I'm not going to church and don't you mention God to me.'

"One night I started to slash my wrists. Flashes of hell came before me. And I cried, 'God, oh, God! Help me!' I threw myself down and said, 'I give you my mandolin, my talent.'

"That night I made Him my Lord, but He wasn't my Savior yet. I still believed you had to be morally good and I thought God was lucky to have me. I was clean on the outside, but inside I was filthy. I had bitterness and pride and a judgmental spirit, especially pride. But I was ignorant and didn't see the need of salvation until God showed me myself as a little girl who was obedient, doing housework, helping mother—a little girl who was trying to get her mother and father's attention.

"I said, 'Oh, God, if you hadn't died for me on the cross, I would go to hell.' I heard a soft voice ask, *What did you say?* I said, 'I would die and go to hell, if you hadn't died for me.'

"I got back to bed and prayed for quite a while and I said, 'Lord, thank You so much!' And he spoke to my heart again and said, *How do you feel?* I felt as though my soul had eaten mints. I never had had that feeling, that assurance before.

"I didn't want to go back to the cold church that hadn't known I was missing. I began visiting churches. Every time, I went away empty.

"Some of the pastors wouldn't talk to me, I think, because they felt a single, divorced woman might cause trouble in the church. I kept searching, believing there was a pastor somewhere who would share with me and help me find healing."

During this time Donna's brother, Scott, the fiddling champion, died from respiratory and cardiac arrest after he drank shaving lotion. Sorrowing over Scott's death, Donna kept searching. Then Jeannie C. Riley told her about the Lord's Chapel. She went to talk with Pastor Moore.

"When I told him my story, Brother Moore said, 'Praise

the Lord. Your family was once our favorite television show. My wife and I would see you dancing and we would pray, "Lord, use that energy for your glory.""

Before she was converted, Donna had sung only with her famous family. Now she could sing about God by herself. At the Lord's Chapel for every service, she drank in the biblical messages and shared her faith with Jeannie C. Riley, Connie Smith, Skeeter Davis, and other believers. Requests began arriving for her to sing and give her testimony. She began going out, "trusting God to provide my needs." She trained herself to use a puppet for children's programs. Named "Sunny Tennessee" the puppet even played the mandolin.

At a Presbyterian church in Virginia, the elders questioned her on doctrine. "They asked me this and that. They wanted to know if I was ordained. I just said, 'I love Jesus." Finally they agreed that I could have the whole service. When the meeting was over, the pastor got up and said, 'I was leary about Donna being here, but she can speak here anytime.'"

Donna didn't ask for any set fee for her ministry: "I accept payment for expenses and whatever love offering they wish to give me. For a long time I was embarrassed to take anything. Every time somebody gave me something, I perspired and shook. Then I went to a home prayer meeting in which 17 people attended. I could tell they were all poor while I was dressed nice. When an old man handed me their love offering of $50, I tried to give it back. 'Sister Donna, don't you dare do that,' he said. 'These people gave from their hearts. You must accept it!

"I go to any church, college, prison,or group that will have me," Donna says. "The denomination doesn't matter. I just share what the Lord has done for me." When music promoters call, she gently explains that she's found a "better Manager."

She tells them and anyone else who inquires: "The life I have now surpasses anything I've ever known, Nothing has ever been so fulfilling as serving Jesus."

Her oldest sister, Grace, sometimes travels with her. The Stoneman brothers and sisters are scattered, but once a year they meet for a weekend family reunion on Sand Mountain in Section, AL. Saturday is taken up with Country music and singing many of the old songs their parents taught them years ago. Sunday morning Donna leads in a worship service. "I hope that one day we can have a family reunion in heaven with Mother and Daddy," she says. "I can't wait to see them again."

Teddy Wilburn: "I didn't trust anyone"

Teddy Wilburn is another Country-music personality who found Christ and who attends the Lord's Chapel. His roots in Country music go about as far back as do Donna Stoneman's.

The second of five children, Teddy started life on a hardscrabble farm in the Arkansas Ozarks. He had three brothers— Doyle, Lester, and Leslie, and one sister, Geraldine. Teddy's father, Benjamin, a disabled World War II veteran, worried that he couldn't support his family by farming and trapping foxes.

Using installment plan from a Kansas City store, Teddy's father in 1937 ordered two guitars, a mandolin, and a ukulele and built a practice platform behind the house., Neighbors began showing up to watch the Wilburn kids perform.

Pop Wilburn mortgaged the farm and bought an old car. For their first professional performance, he drove the family to Thayer, MO. In the courthouse square Teddy and Doyle, ages 6 and 7, pulled their instruments from flour sacks and struck up a song. Pop passed the hat and collected six dollars and 40 cents.

The kids performed in one-room schools and churches; their parents sold tickets for 15 to 20 cents a show. They sang on the radio for the first time in Jonesboro, AR. Then trouble struck. Teddy developed tuberculosis. Their house burned down; they were forced to move into a chicken coop.

When Pop Wilburn heard that Roy Acuff was judging a talent contest in Birmingham, he packed the family into the car. They arrived in a rainstorm just as the winners were being announced. "We'll go around to the stage door and catch Roy when he's coming out," the father said. When Roy emerged, they started singing in the rain. "We must have been a sad sight," Teddy recalls, "because Roy cried."

Roy got them on the Opry. Then after six months they were forced off because of child-labor laws. Returning to Arkansas they continued performing wherever they could draw a crowd. Pop Wilburn had picture cards printed of the family and the children sold them for a nickel apiece. For a while they moved to Hot Springs, AR, and lived in a shed and one room of a tourist court.

In 1948 the family joined the Louisiana Hayride in Shreveport, performing Saturday nights and doing a weekday radio show just ahead of Hank Williams. During their stay of three years Pop helped launch the music career of Webb Pierce, a young manager of the shirt department at the local Sears Roebuck store. A young 9-year-old singer named Brenda Lee was also featured on the Wilburns' show.

The Wilburn Brothers, as Teddy and Doyle were known, became a highly successful act. Showcased on American Bandstand and other national television shows, they recorded one hit after another. The biggest was *Trouble's Back in Town*, which was voted "Country Record of the Year" in the 1962 *Cash Box* year-end poll. They also toured across the U.S. and into Canada and in Europe.

Pop Wilburn died in 1965. "Daddy was a very good man," Teddy recalls. "Very stern and hard, though. He didn't know how to express himself. Love was not expressed in our home. It was taken for granted. I don't know what his relationship with God was when he left."

Brothers Lester and Leslie joined Teddy and Doyle in music-related business ventures; sister Geraldine got married. Their song-publishing company multiplied to four corporations with the brothers serving as producers, booking agents, and managers for many of the biggest names in the business.

They gave a contract to Loretta Lynn, the young singer from Butcher Hollow, KY. Under Teddy and Doyle's guidance Loretta became a superstar; then after 10 years she broke away. In her book, *Coal Miner's Daughter*, Loretta talks about their relationship, but their involvement in her career isn't mentioned in her smash movie. Says Teddy, "We spent 10 years of our lives eating, breathing, and sleeping the act of Loretta Lynn. When I read the movie script, I saw that it barely touched on us. I asked them to just take us out. But it's an excellent movie."

The break with Loretta hurt Teddy Wilburn deeply: "I just about gave up on humanity," Teddy recalls. "I vowed to never help another living human being as long as I lived. I filled myself up with bitterness, hatred, and distrust. I became a heavy drinker and so paranoid that I didn't trust anyone.

"I remember seeing *The Exorcist* movie and asking a couple of friends if they thought I was no longer Teddy. I had become someone I didn't like. I totally hated everything I represented."

Teddy had never been one to share his problems with people. However, he did respect Skeeter Davis and a few others in the music community. In February 1976 he consented to go with Skeeter to the Lord's chapel. At the last minute Skeeter was called to Louisville for a television show and urged him to "please go on anyway. You'll love it."

As a boy back in Arkansas Teddy had joined a Baptist church but hadn't attended in years. He ran into May Axton, the mother of a friend in the music business and asked her to go with him to the Lord's Chapel.

When they arrived at the Lord's Chapter, Billy Ray Moore was inviting people to seek personal counseling. "Will you go with me?" Teddy asked May. Together they talked with an elder about Teddy's troubles. "The elder quoted Scripture—I can't remember what," Teddy says. "And he prayed, but nothing happened to me until three or four days later.

"I became afraid someone was going to kill me. In this frame of mind I called a doctor friend and asked if I could stop by his house. When I got there, my body started shaking uncontrollably. Then God spoke to me and said, 'I'm preparing you for death.' I started crying, for I was afraid I would die that night. God said, 'Not tonight. I'm preparing you for when you do die.' Scriptures started pouring out of my mouth like I had become a preacher. I kept telling the doctor, 'Listen to what the Bible says' and 'I'm being saved!'

"Something like an electric shock ran through my body from head to toe. It happened twice. Holding a *Living Bible* I left the doctor at the door of his apartment.

"I sang hymns all the way home, The lines made sense to me for the first time in my life. Then doubts started coming. Satan tried to tell me that he and not God had given me that experience. I said, 'Hold on, there, Satan. You can't tell me how you would make me feel that way.' I had experienced the most beautiful feeling that I will ever have this side of heaven. I said, 'Dear God, please show me that was from You and not from Satan.' And that same beautiful feeling swept through my body for the second time.

"When I got home, I just opened the Bible and started reading. My eyes hit the page at Psalm 60. I don't know where I went from there. I was in and out of bed all night long. I was asking for forgiveness for treating people the way I had. I remember getting up the next morning and telling my mother what had happened. I said, 'Mother, where did all the hate go and where did all this love come from?'"

Later Teddy became able to discern what had happened. He says: "I can identify with Paul and his experience on the road to Damascus. I'm sure some people will not understand what occurred to me, but if you have ever lived in the depths of hell on earth as I did, you have no way of explaining how it is when you have been lifted out of that pit by God's hand.

"I'm still learning to love and trust people. I still don't open up with fellow Christians as much as I should. I do talk to God a lot, basically because I know he and I are the only two that can do anything about my problems."

Teddy retains his boyish face and twinkling blue eyes. Teddy wants to believe that his deceased show-business friends are in heaven: "Red Foley was touched by God. No doubt about that. So were Elvis Presley and Hank Williams. They touched so many people, especially Hank with *I Saw the Light*. Hank had to have spiritual help in putting the words down to that song.

"Samson went on his own way and suffered. God still came back to him in the end. That is so beautiful. Maybe it was that way with Elvis and Hank and my daddy. I think there are mysteries of God that you and I still don't know, things that He keeps to Himself.

"We shouldn't be too quick to judge. That's one reason I love the Lord's Chapel. We try to accept and love one another. We should because look how much God loves us."

The Coal-Miner's Son

Billy Grammer is a big, square-shouldered man with a friendly grin and hair turning silver. The drums and cymbals are quiet as he eases his lips up close to the microphone. "Folks, I'd like to do one of the oldtimers that's real Country music. See how you like it." The song is the timeless *I Was Seeing Nellie Home*. When he's through, the applause is loud and long until he does another stanza.

Billy is talking to me backstage at the Opry. "People love the old songs. They're scared to death for the old traditional music. Who would ever think that [my rendition of] *Nellie* would get six encores on the Opry during the last three months?"

One of the world's top guitarists as well as a vocalist, Billy remains one of the most beloved Country performers, although he now is semi-retired from the profession. As a Tennessee fan puts it, "Billy Grammer's as solid as Gibraltar. He stands for something and doesn't move with every change of the wind."

Billy is quick to give God all the credit: "If it wasn't for the Lord, I'd still be out there boozing, chasing, and gambling. The people who know me best know who I was and who I am today. They know the change in my life has to be from the Lord."

Billy Grammer could be termed the "coal-miner's son." The oldest of nine brothers and four sisters, he grew up in the mining country of southern Illinois. His father, who worked in the deep mines for 36 years, died at age 56 from leukemia and black lung disease.

"We never knew whether Dad would be coming home," Billy recalls. "He was in three major explosions where miners were killed. I once asked him after one if he was scared. He said, 'Well, a little bit, son.'

""Did you run?'

"No, but I passed some boys that did."

Billy continues to reminisce. "We had a 40-acre farm that wouldn't grow anything but kids, persimmon sprouts, sassafras bushes, and a little corn and soybeans. We weren't different from our neighbors. Everybody worked and helped each other. If somebody's barn burned, the community put up another one. Same with a house. We didn't worry about being poor. We had plenty to eat and a roof to keep rain off us. And the Wabash River to lay a trot line in.

"We had strict discipline at school and at home," Billy says. "When dad whistled, kids would fall out of trees and head for the house. It was partly out of fear, yes, but we also respected him. When he did whip one of us, we knew he had a reason. He never beat us up."

Billy also respected his father as a violinist and fiddle player. "Dad had two years in the Army school of music. He farmed and worked in the mines. He didn't follow the music business because he didn't want to be around drinkers.

"I was reared hearing and playing all kinds of music, from light classics like *Humoresque* and *The Blue Danube Waltz* to Country favorites such as *The Eighth of January* and *Sally Good'un*. Name them; I can play them. I learned them in the home. Dad played the fiddle and I accompanied him on the guitar. Then as I got older, I played with him at pie suppers and school and church functions.

Billy married his high-school sweetheart, Ruth Burzynski, a coal-miner's daughter and also one of 13 children. "The whole country threw their hands up when Ruth and I got married," Billy laughs. "I think they thought we'd have 26 kids. We have only three, but those three have more than 70 first cousins!"

After a short stretch in the Army near the end of World

War II, Billy hitchhiked to Arlington, VA, auditioned, and got a job as vocalist and band leader of Connie B. Gay's Radio Ranchmen on WARL. Billy says, "It was like the old saying, 'Yesterday I couldn't spell *entertainer*. Today I are one.'"

For three-and-a-half years Billy worked with Jimmy Dean, Grandpa Jones, Hawkshaw Hawkins, and other performers in the Washington DC area. Then he struck gold with a million-selling record, *Gotta Travel On*, which propelled him straight to the Opry.

When he was 16 Billy made a profession of faith and was baptized in a Baptist church in Illinois. When he and Ruth moved to Nashville, they transferred their membership to a church there. Billy never attended after he joined. He preferred the lifestyle he had been following in the music world.

"I cussed, gambled, and drank more booze than you could stack in a room," Billy admits. "I wasn't an alcoholic—yet. I could drink a fifth of vodka on the rocks and still be on my feet. The boys that worked with me wouldn't even know I'd been drinking."

Home for Billy became just a place to unwind between trips and to park his silver boots. "Ruth and our three children were awfully patient with me," he concedes. "They had to put up with an awful lot."

When Billy and Ruth's first grandchild was born with irreparable birth defects, Billy noticed that his family was sustained by a deep, inner peace which he lacked. During that same time he was going through entrance rites for the Masonic Lodge. One question the group asked him was: "On whom do you put your trust?"

Billy replied, "In God." Afterward he realized that he had lied. "I knew I wasn't putting my trust in anybody other than myself. This bothered me."

The following September Bob Harrington, the self-styled

Chaplain of Bourbon Street, held a crusade in Nashville. Relatives visiting the Grammers urged Billy to go with them to hear Harrington. Billy had planned on going bass fishing that night, but a prop on his motor was broken, so he went to the service. Ruth then was quite concerned about their 16-year-old son, William Archie. "Make him go with us," she told her husband.

"That would be the kettle calling the pot black," Billy replied, "but I'll see that he goes." The boy went but sat away from his family in another part of the auditorium." As the colorful Harrington preached that night, Billy silently mocked him. Then the mocking turned to irritation: *Why is this preacher picking on me when I'm already church member?* But when the preacher gave the invitation to accept Christ, Billy went forward. At the front of the auditorium he saw his 16-year-old son. Neither had known the other was going to respond.

Billy's son became a Christian. Billy rededicated his life to Christ and changed radically. He quit drinking and cursing, began reading the Bible and praying regularly, and shared his faith with almost everyone he met. Three weeks later he put down his Bible and said, "Ruth, the Lord just brought to my attention that I was not saved before. For the first time in my life I have an awareness of Christ in my life."

The following week Billy got a call from Bob Harrington: "I have a crusade going in Chattanooga and have to be away one night. Will you be the preacher?"

"I wouldn't know what to do," Billy countered.

"I know you won't, but the Lord will. Just give your testimony and preside. Others will be giving their testimonies, too. You won't have to talk long."

Billy went and did as he was asked to do. About a dozen people accepted the Lord that night.

Billy's son, William Archie, already was active with Campus

Crusade for Christ in high school. Crusade workers asked Billy to help with a Country-music program at Crusade headquarters in Arrowhead Springs, CA. Billy went, but a mixup on the dates occurred. He prepared to return home.

A Crusade leader caught up with Billy as he was packing to leave. He apologized for the confusion and persuaded Billy to remain a couple of days for Crusade's Lay Institute. "I'll always be glad I stayed," says Billy. "They taught me how to win people to Christ without strong-arming them."

In 1972 Billy was performing on the grandstand at a shopping center in Laurel, MD, when he heard a shot ring out. Alabama Governor George Wallace had just been cut down in an assassination attempt by Arthur H. Bremer.

Billy ran to Wallace's side, knelt to pray, then stood to give reassurance to the crowd. Television anchor Walter Cronkite later credited Billy with bringing the angry crowd under control.

For a while Billy wrestled with the idea that God might be calling him to full-time ministry. He soon saw that he had "a unique opportunity to be a witness in the music business. I realized that every saved person is a minister, though some are set apart as pastors, evangelists, and teachers. God doesn't say, 'Go to this place or that place' as much as He says, 'As you're going, be my witnesses.'

"A guy would come up and ask me, 'What's new?' I'd say, 'Come over here and I'll tell you what's new with me.' I found that it was best not to witness to someone in front of a crowd of people."

When Billy decided not to perform in nightclubs anymore, a friend in the music business warned, "You're getting ready to starve to death." Billy replied, "I've inherited the universe, Chief, so let me starve."

"He looked at me," Billy says, "as if I'd flipped my lid.

"Booking agents did tempt me a while with nightclub

engagements. When one called, I didn't go into big details but just said, 'My convictions have taken me out of such places. Thanks for calling me.'"

Billy knows a lot of "lovable boys and girls in the music business who would like to break away from booze and the nightclub and honkytonk circuit. They're in a rat race. They're trapped. They'd love to get out of it. They don't realize that they won't break away until the Holy Spirit gets to them."

Another result of Billy's conversion is a deeper relationship with Ruth and their children. All three of the kids are Christians. William Archie is a minister, as is one of their sons-in-law.

"The Lord has been good to me and my family," Billy declares. "All of us intend to keep on serving Him."

As they grew older in the 1980s, Billy and Ruth built a log cabin near Sesser, IL, and moved there from Nashville. Billy's eyes are troubling him, but he still can play the guitar.

This "coal-miner's son" is not ready to quit, for music is in his blood. "Once you walk the high wire, you continue to walk the high wire," he says.

For Billy Grammer and many other Country performers, ministry is more important than music.

Chapter 10
Stars with Faith

Cynics in Nashville, Branson, Austin, and other Country-music centers say the number of "real" Christians in the profession can be counted on one hand. As one preacher puts things sarcastically, the rest turn to God when their marriages break up, when they can't whip drug habits, or when they haven't had a hit in 10 years. Then one can find dreamy-eyed fans who expect hillbilly heaven to welcome everyone who ever picked up a guitar or a fiddle. The cynics judge too quickly. Country-music Christians aren't perfect, on stage or off. They are from different religious backgrounds but share many of the same struggles. Here are the stories of some who are cut from different molds.

Wilma Lee Cooper:
Real Country with Real Values

The Cooper name is synonymous with old-time mountain ballads and gospel songs. The Library of Music at Harvard named Wilma Lee, her late husband Stoney, and their "Clinch Mountain Clan" the "most authentic mountain singing group in America." When you hear her and the "Clan" lifting the rafters with *He Will Set Your Fields on Fire* and *Blessed Jesus, Hold My Hand,* you know that is true. You can almost hear the home folks clapping in her childhood Assembly of God church back in West Virginia.

The oldest of three Leary girls, Wilma Lee started singing Country gospel and the old ballads with her family at home. Neighbors began dropping by. Soon the family had invitations to sing in churches and schools.

When an uncle in their group went back to teaching school, Wilma Lee's father substituted a young fiddler he had heard over the radio. "Fiddlin' Dale" Cooper also was from a devout family. The Learys called him "Stoney". He and Wilma Lee fell in love and were married in 1941.

When daughter Carol Lee was born, they quit the music business. They didn't think performing went with good parenthood. Wilma Lee stayed home while Stoney delivered Soda pop. Soon tiring of this routine they took a job in Nebraska doing six radio programs a day. Two of their most frequently requested songs were *Wreck on the Highway* and *Don't Make Me Go to Bed and I'll Be Good.*

During the next 16 years they traveled 100,000 miles a year. In 1957 they joined the Grand Ole Opry. Their records began climbing the charts.

Wilma Lee and Stoney faithfully attended an Assembly of God church in Nashville. The fidelity of their marriage relationship was the envy of their colleagues. One hardly was ever seen without the other.

Then after 20 years on the Opry, Stoney suffered a fatal heart attack. Fellow entertainer Vic Willis remembers him as "one of the finest, most decent persons I've ever met. He was always concerned about other people's problems."

"Stoney", declares Grandpa Jones, "was a very religious man. Everybody liked him. He was quiet, but when he got up before an audience, he always had something to say." Roy Acuff pronounces Stoney "the most humble man I ever met."

"Above all, Stoney was a Christian," Wilma Lee says with

certainty. "I don't worry about where he is now. He would want me to keep on." So she continues performing on the Opry stage. Sometimes she and Carol Lee do duets.

After being divorced from Jimmie Snow, daughter Carol married a staff musician of the Opry. She has her own backup group, "The Carol Lee Singers", which goes on stage for almost every Opry performance. They also serve as recording-session musicians for some of the biggest names in the business. Carol and her family attend the Assembly of God Church in Brentwood, TN.

Neither Wilma Lee nor Carol looks her age. At 70 Wilma Lee retains her girlish looks and a strong voice. She is still partial to the old songs of the heart and faith she learned from her parents in West Virginia.

Larry Gatlin: "They Used to Take Up a Collection in Church to Get Me to Shut Up"

This native Texan cut his teeth on shaped-note gospel songs and the backs of Pentecostal pews. His mother entered him a talent contest when he was only 6-years old. Later he sang with younger brothers Steve and Rudy and sister LaDonna in a family gospel quartet, with Mother Gatlin accompanying them on the piano.

Dad Gatlin was an oil driller whose work took him all over Texas. The family went along and sang in churches wherever the Gatlins happened to be living. Larry emceed the show. Never at a loss for words he says, "They used to take up a collection in church just to get me to shut up."

Only five-feet, eight-inches tall, Larry quarterbacked his football team in high school and at the University of Houston.

"I was the smallest one on my team and always a little cocky," he admits.

After he graduated from the university, Larry attended law school briefly and then headed for Las Vegas, where he hoped to sing in Elvis Presley's backup group. Opry star Dottie West heard him and was so impressed that she sent him a plane ticket for Nashville. When he arrived, she introduced him to Johnny Cash, Kris Kristofferson, and other influentials. Confident of success Larry told them, "The Lord wants me to write and sing songs. That's why I'm here."

His sister, LaDonna, got married and joined the David Wilkerson evangelistic team. Brothers Steve and Rudy followed Larry to Nashville and have remained with him ever since. "They're the finest two human beings I know," Larry says. "One is my right hand; the other's my left."

Larry married and had a child, Kristen, named after his friend, Kris Kristofferson. One day while he was driving, Larry had a bad daydream of what Kristen might grow up to be. As a result he wrote *Penny Annie*, a song about a pretty little girl who grew up to be a drug addict and a prostitute.

Larry typically writes message songs with heavy biblical overtones. *Those Also Love* says that the "beautiful people" aren't the only ones who fall in love. *Help Me*, written for Johnny Cash's movie, "The Gospel Road", is a sinking man's prayer.

One evening Larry and Dottie West went to the Union Mission where Merle Haggard was recording an album titled "Land of Many Churches." After observing the homeless derelicts, Larry wrote and recorded with his brothers his most controversial song. *Midnight Choir* is about a group of bums who straggle into the mission for supper and then wander back to the street to find a bottle of wine. They pray that they'll find Mogen David [wine] in heaven." If it's not, "who the hell wants to go?" say the song lyrics.

The song brought Larry and his brothers a pile of protest

mail accusing them of being sacrilegious and of making sick jokes about derelicts. Even though they offered to donate their royalties from the song to rescue missions, the complaints kept arriving. They finally sent a letter of apology to radio stations. They expressed sorrow if *Midnight Choir* had caused any problems. But they were "not sorry that we released the record. We searched our hearts and did what we thought we had to do . . . God help the wino . . .; [it] doesn't look like anyone else is going to!"

"No Billy Graham", Larry says his calling is to "sit on a stool and sing songs that I hope ring true."

Larry is quick to criticize hypocrisy and pretense. "Lots of people are trying to be religious because the thing to do is to see and be seen. I hate to go to church on Easter because all I see are the new hats and outfits."

Larry told interviewer David Graham: "They should take the robes off the choir and the preacher and quit reading prayers and sermons. So many preachers don't preach out of the Bible but just throw a little in . . . Faith comes by hearing the Word of God."

His theology can hardly be faulted. He expounds on grace as "someone loving you when you have nothing to offer in return. That's God. Religion is man-made." Still, he sometimes offends sensitivities by using mild profanity in press interviews.

On the road Larry Gatlin is one of the strictest entertainers in the business. He allows neither narcotics nor alcohol on his bus. He tells a musician desiring a job in his band: "If you have to get high to play our music, you're the wrong guy."

In a typical show Larry and his brothers lead off with a couple of songs; then he says, "Folks, we've invited you into our living room. We're gonna do the best we can for you. If you'll listen with your ears and eyes and heart and soul, we'll all have a good time." Larry offers a standing money-back guarantee, which no fan has taken him up on yet. He also never hesitates to tell a heckler or a drunk disturbing his performance to leave.

The outlaw image projected by some Country singers is commercially motivated, Larry says. Rhinestones don't appeal to the Gatlin brothers either. The typical Gatlin garb consists of jeans, open shirts, and maybe vests. "We don't wear claws or white eye shadow," Larry says. "Women don't throw their panties and room keys on our stage either. We're good guys."

Larry lives with wife Janice and their children, 17-year-old daughter Kristen and 13-year-old son Joshua Cash, in a 150-year-old log house on an 84-acre farm in Antioch, TN, a little south of Nashville.

Larry refuses to bend his convictions: "I owe my children more than seeing their daddy busted on a narcotics charge. At least my kids can say their daddy stood for something."

Besides his family Larry's greatest joy is in helping people through his songs. One evening after a performance a fan walked up and said, "My wife and daughter were killed a year ago in a car accident. If it hadn't been for your songs, *Help Me, Light through the Darkness,* and *Mercy River,* I think I would have lost my mind." Larry hugged the man.

"That's where it's at," Larry Gatlin declares. "Having a God-given talent with which to touch and help others is more precious than gold. That's what we're here for."

Barbara Mandrell: "The Beauty of Country Music Is That It Talks about Real People"

Larry Gatlin's female counterpart, in many ways, is superstar Barbara Mandrell, a 5-foot-2, 95-pound scrapper. Sisters Louise and Irline are almost as well-known as Barbara. Like the Gatlins, the Mandrell sisters were reared in a Pentecostal church on hand-clapping, foot-stomping gospel music. "The Lord has always been a part of my family and my growing up," says Barbara, who is happily married with three children. She and Larry are near the same age. Both her career and his skyrocketed at about the same time. A "Snow White" (the title given her by *People* magazine) in her personal life, she parallels Larry both in religious devotion and the raise eyebrows she gets from a few of her songs.

Barbara sounded her first note on Christmas Day in Houston. At age 5 she learned how to play the accordion and quickly mastered the saxophone and the guitar.

"We had a problem trying to get her not to practice," says her father, Irby. "We had to make her go outside and play with other kids."

When she did play, she preferred the boys' teams. In high school she was the champion "burn-out" baseball player—a game in which two gloved players see who can slam the hardest ball at each other.

At age 12 Barbara was "discovered" by Joe Maphis at a musical-instrument fair in Chicago, where she was demonstrating drums, Maphis took her to Las Vegas for her debut as a professional performer.

After she turned 13, the child prodigy sang with father Irby Mandrell and became a regular on the Town Hall Party television show in Los Angeles. She also toured with Johnny Cash, Red Foley, and Patsy Cline and did several overseas junkets.

At age 14 she fell in love with Ken Dudney, the new drummer her father had hired for the family band. She dated six other men (five proposed!) before turning 18 and marrying ex-drummer Dudney, who had become a Navy pilot.

Happily wed, she quit mosaic and moved with Ken to Washington, DC. She taught Sunday school at the base chapel and had plans of being simply a wife and mother. When Ken got orders for overseas, she decided to wait out his duty with her parents, who had moved to Nashville.

One evening she and her father took in the Opry. Sitting in the audience she became restless. "I belong up there," she told Irby. She soon got back in the business.

In 1972 she became an Opry regular. Her first recordings—*I've Been Loving You Too Long to Stop Now, Mama Don't Allow No Music Playing Around Here,* and *Do Right, Woman, Do Right, Man*—got plenty of attention. In 1973 she hit big with *Midnight Oil.* Six years later the Academy of Country Music voted her Entertainer of the Year.

With a girlish, impish smile Barbara now performs on the biggest stages and the highest-rated television variety shows in the nation. Only Dolly Parton and Loretta Lynn among female Country stars are in her league. With all her fame, Barbara is still, by music writer Don Rhodes' estimate, "one of the most religious, clean-talking, straight-living, people-loving, kind-acting persons I've ever met."

For Barbara, career and family are intertwined. Her father, Irby, is show manager and travels with Barbara and the "Do-Rites" band, named for her song *Do Right, Woman, Do Right, Man.* Her mother makes all of her costumes. Husband Ken, who once served as official pilot for the governor of Tennessee, deals with the finances.

Any woman who lives with a man outside of marriage is "stupid", according to Barbara, who terms herself a "pro-America everything." She permits her band members neither drugs or alcohol and no women in their motel rooms.

Barbara is also strict about the magazines in her house and turned down requests for an interview with *Playboy.*

Barbara and Ken have no rules about household chores. "We don't have ego problems because he's not insecure," she says. "His job is just as prestigious as mine and he loves his work as much as I love mine." While admitting ups and downs in their relationship she says their marriage has been a success. Her worst ordeal resulted from a traffic accident. Driving with her son, Matthew, and daughter, Jamie, outside Nashville, Barbara's car was hit headon by another car. Usually she disdained seatbelts. This time the belts saved their lives. The driver of the other car was killed.

Metal pins and surgery repaired her broken leg. A legal technicality required that she sue the dead driver's estate. This brought a torrent of bad publicity. Battered both emotionally and physically she struggled back with the support of her family. She eventually resumed her career and even had a third child.

The Mandrells live in a northern Nashville suburb and have vacation homes in Colorado and Alabama. Sisters Irline and Louise visit Barbara and Ken often.

Barbara says her Christian faith is as strong as ever. "I can't sing gospel songs and not mean them. It has to be a part of me. My belief in God and my Christian life are very real."

Barbara is displeased with press articles suggesting she has traded her clean, Country-girl image for a sexy-flashy one. At least one of her Christian performer friends has talked to her about singing songs which seem to justify immorality. *If Loving You Is Wrong, I Don't Want to Be Right* was targeted. "Barbara, that isn't the kind of song that's good for you," he suggested.

Barbara has turned down some songs, changed others with distasteful lyrics, and refuses to sing profanity. Some of her songs, she admits, do not reflect her personal life. "I've never had anyone take my husband away," she told music critic Alanna Nash. "The beauty of Country music is that it talks about real people."

Barbara doesn't plan on always being a performer. "When I reach the top and start to go the other way, then I'll be through. I'll know when I reach it."

George Hamilton IV: "Forever Young"

The Country folk songs of George Hamilton IV create no controversy. The lanky balladeer, born in 1939 and reared in a Baptist church in North Carolina, says flatly, "Cheatin' and drinkin' songs are not my material."

What George does enjoy singing are old-time, heart-tugging ballads, upbeat love songs, and patriotic music. His first big hit, recorded when he was a freshman at the University of North Carolina, was titled, *A Rose and Baby Ruth*. It sold more than a million copies. Other hits were *Early Morning Rain, Abilene, That's What You Get for Loving Me,* and *Forever Young.*

In Europe George long has been the most popular American Country-music entertainer. Overseas writers call George "an American hillbilly." He grew up in a suburb of Winston-Salem, NC, where he and his grandfather listened to the Grand Ole Opry every Saturday night over the radio. George became a devoted fan of Ernest Tubb, Roy Acuff, Hank Williams, and other greats.

When George was 12, he saved his earnings from a paper route and persuaded his parents to let him see the Opry. His mother called ahead to friends in Nashville and pinned a note to his coat to identify him in case of a mixup. The trip was the highlight of his early youth.

After high-school graduation George enrolled as a broadcasting major at the University of North Carolina, where he met songwriter John D. Loudermilk and promoter Orville Campbell, the man who discovered Andy Griffith. With *A*

Rose and Baby Ruth they turned the thin Carolinian into a celebrity. George later moved to Washington to be on Jimmy Dean's television show and finished his studies at American University

On a trip home he married "Tinky", his high-school sweetheart—"the most thrilling experience of my life." They have two sons and a daughter; the oldest son is George Hamilton V.

From Washington George and Tinky moved to Nashville, where Chet Atkins recorded him on RCA. George joined the Grand Ole Opry and began making overseas tours. In 1971 George, Loretta Lynn, and the Glaser Brothers were named winners of Billboard's first annual international Country-music award.

George and Tinky became homesick for North Carolina. They decided to move back, even though this meant George would have to leave the Opry.

About a year later George was invited to do a television show for the British Broadcasting Corporation. That led to five more shows and a weekly television series in Canada. When he was in London again, he gave a lecture on American Country music to foreign guests at the American Embassy.

Alone with his guitar on a bare stage he chatted about the origins of Country music in the United States. He picked and sang the ballads *Greensleeves* and *Barbara Allen* and talked about how Johnny Cash is a direct descendant of the troubadours.

Representatives of the Soviet and Czech governments were at the embassy and invited him to Moscow and Prague. He became the first American Country-music entertainer to perform in what was then the socialist bloc of European nations.

A Czech string band greeted him at the Prague airport. They took him to a hall where the director handed over a list of songs the group had been rehearsing. Every song on the list, including *The Family Bible*, was a George Hamilton special. He did four evening performances before packed houses—a total of 28,000 people.

In Prague he was asked whether his family was related in any way to the Czechoslovakian people. He told them about the Moravians in North Carolina, who had hailed from what later became known as Czechoslovakia. That disclosure led to a visit with the Moravian bishop in Prague. At a Moravian church service he sang *Amazing Grace* for a congregation of about 30 who never had heard it. Before he left the small church, he talked to two young people who told him that to join the church they had to fill out papers barring them from college. "I was ashamed of ever griping about getting up and going to church on Sunday morning," he said later.

He repeated his lecture-concert at the Soviet Institute of Foreign Languages, where 250 students, speaking fluent English, heard him. After a while the woman choir director said, "We'd like to sing with you."

"I don't know any Russian songs," George admitted.

"We can sing your songs," she smiled. When they began singing *This Land Is Your Land*, the chill bumps rose on George's back. They sang about *Someone's in the Kitchen with Dinah* and *Working on the Railroad*. Then the choir director said hesitantly, "I know a good song, but you might not like it."

"Go ahead," George grinned. The students sang, "We're goin' to lay down our atom bombs down by the riverside." Again the American visitor was deeply touched.

When the time was up, the choir director thanked him. "This was so beautiful," she said to George. "The songs came from your heart and from our hearts."

In 1976 the Opry changed its rules and permitted George

to commute to Nashville from North Carolina. George's American music career began picking up again. After 10 years of commuting, he and Tinky sold their home in Matthews, NC, and moved to a restored farmhouse 30 miles south of Nashville near Franklin, TN. Here they became active in the Oak Valley Baptist Church, to which several other Country-music personalities belong.

George Hamilton IV and his son, George V frequently team up for old and new folksy favorites and gospel classics such as *Using My Bible for a Roadmap* and *Build Me a Cabin in Gloryland.* George recently recalled to his son a music lesson: "I scribbled three chords down on a piece of paper, briefly demonstrating the finger positions, and then you were off alone to your room to practice. That was it—my entire contribution to your musical future."

George performs for Christian groups as much as possible. "There's a better chance today for a religious revival then there has ever been," he says. "Youth are searching for what is real."

Stu Phillips: "Born to Be a Man"

If George Hamilton IV dampens the hillbilly stereotype of Country singers, then Stu Phillips shatters it. Stu is a cultured, college-educated Canadian from Montreal by way of Edmonton and Calgary, Alberta. He is both a member of the Grand Ole Opry and an ordained Episcopal priest.

Smartly attired ina tailored suit and open white shirt (and sometimes in full tux), he stands just behind the colored footlights of the Opry stage. With the microphone held close to his lips he croons a number from his newest album: "born to be a man . . . Born to really live . . . To have a wife . . . To spend my life . . . A daddy born to give . . . ." Then he sings about life

174

having more to it "than drinking beer out of a can . . . more than getting high . . .." The crowd loves his soul-lifting song, which praise marital and family love. Says Stu: "My album, Born to Be a Man, pretty much sounds like the philosophical tone of my life. I like songs that express in a wholesome way the aspirations of the human heart. That's what Country music is. That's why people relate to it so well. It's just the expression of the human heart."

On Sunday mornings Stu Phillips dons white clerical collar, surplice, and robe. He speaks softly and conversationally and looks directly at the congregation with his familiar twinkle and smile. You almost expect him to break into a ballad as he begins his message.

Last Sunday I was resting in the guest room of a home and happened to see four parachutes drifting down. A few minutes later I saw four more and then another four. We talked about that during dinner time and about courage and confidence. My host said, "You probably understand that skydiving is based more on faith than courage."

Faith is an important word in skydiving and in all of life. I heard of a skydiver who was told, "Just pull the ripcord. Don't worry about a thing. When you hit the ground, there'll be a truck to pick you up." Well, the young man jumped, counted to 10, pulled the cord, and nothing happened. He looked back at the plane and shook his fist. "They probably forgot to send the truck, too," he yelled.

My [stuttering friend] Mel Tillis said he would have a problem as a skydiver and counting "wo-wo-wo-one . .

ta-ta-ta-two."

Continuing his message Stu describes faith as falling free into the arms of God's love. Does God ask us to take a leap without anything to go on, with no assurance of promises fulfilled? No, certainly not. Having drawn his audience into the heart of his message he begins expounding on the story of God's calling Abraham to offer his son Isaac as a sacrifice. "Abraham," Stu notes,

responded to God in total obedience. He didn't question God. He obeyed. Our duty is to believe and trust God, to love and obey him, to bring others to know him, to put nothing in his place, to show him respect in song, word, and deed, to set aside regular times for study, worship, and prayer.

We have a duty and responsibility, Stu says, to work; to pray for peace; to bear no malice, prejudice, or hate in our hearts; to be kind to all God's creatures; to use all our bodily desires as God intends; to be honest and fair in our dealings; to seek justice and freedom for all people; and to use our talents and possessions in God's service.

That's quite a list. We can't do it by ourselves. We need the outside help that comes through Christ's vicarious atonement. The essence of Abraham faith is imparted to all through Christ . . .

This brings us to making a commitment, jumping out of the airplane, becoming an active participant . . .
The abundant life, the promise of the Lord, this is ours

the moment we receive Christ. Jesus asks us to make a commitment to Him, to recognize the true value of riches that endure forever . . .

The message is vintage Stu Phillips.

Stu is committed to the same evangelical faith which his Pentecostal and Baptist friends hold. "There has never been a time in my life," he declares, "when God didn't have his hand on me, yet over the past several years a change has come into my life which I believe is the work of the Holy Spirit. Certain things are more important to me. I'm more relaxed. I know that God has his hand on me more than ever."

Stu's father was an architect in Montreal. "We grew up as Anglicans surrounded by Roman Catholics," Stu recalls. "Our church, St. George's, is one of the oldest churches in Montreal. My parents were there every time the doors opened. I was an acolyte, started in the boys' choir when 6 or 7, and later taught Sunday school. I also became a lay elder and an usher. Even when I couldn't attend, I always kept a close association with my church."

Stu became involved in music early. At age 8 he bought his own guitar for $850 and taught himself to play. Idolizing Gene Autry he fantasized riding the Western ranges to challenge the bad men.

When Stu was 13, Gene Autry visited Montreal for a rodeo and amateur talent contest. Stu entered the singing competition and won first prize—$15. The officials were so impressed that they took up a collection which netted Stu a total of $150.

After he attended Sir George Williams College in Montreal, he moved to the Western prairies and worked as a radio announcer for CFRN, Edmonton, Alberta. He did the sing-on program, Stu for Breakfast, on weekday mornings, as well as station breaks and commercials for other programs. Sunday mornings, when he had to work, he listened to ministers of every denomination. "Even there," he recalls, "God had his hand on my life."

Named the outstanding announcer for Edmonton, he advanced to emceeing a weekly two-hour talent show, produced The Canadian Opry, and arranged many other variety shows. One summer he filled in as a replacement for the star of Finian's Rainbow. While in Edmonton he met his future wife, Aldona, a Lithuanian girl from the Alberta prairies.

In 1962 Stu went national with a cowboy variety show on television. For the next five years he starred on his own Red River Jamboree over the Canadian Broadcasting Corporation network. Wearing a Stetson, fancy boots, and a pair of six guns for the role, he did rope tricks with his horse, Nugget. During this time he traveled coast to coast in both the United States and Canada and appeared on the Opry in Nashville about 40 times.

The CBC offered him a dream lifetime contract. He turned it down "because I felt the time had come to change my cowboy image. I remember distinctly taking my hat off for the last time, pulling my boots off, and hanging up my gunbelts. I've never worn a ten-gallon hat or guns since."

Joining the Opry in 1967 Stu moved to Nashville with Aldona and their two children. A third child was born after they arrived in Opry town.

He tries to keep his ecclesiastical and entertaining roles separate: "In the church and on the Opry I try to do everything for the glory of God. I'll go along with being introduced as an Episcopal worker priest. But I don't think it's my place to say, 'Well, folks, as long as I've got you here, open your Bibles to such and such.'

"I believe you can impose on people to the detriment of

the Word. One of the greatest mistakes in history occurred when Constantine declared Christianity to be the official religion of the Roman Empire. People didn't really change. They just fell into a folk culture.

"What's important is that my fans know my spiritual position and that my church knows my music position. I don't think anyone should use the Lord for show business."

Wilma Lee Cooper, Larry Gatlin, Barbara Mandrell, George Hamilton IV, and Stu Phillips all are stellar Country-music entertainers. Reared in Christian homes they practice their faith both on stage and off.

Chapter 11
Heartaches and Life Changes

Country-music folks—writers, singers, pickers, fiddlers, and other talents—do a lot of brainstorming together. On this special evening in Nashville songwriters Marijohn Wilkin and John Loudermilk are trying to dream up a new song. They'd like to be a hit.

A Rising Songwriter

John is sprawled on the floor. Marijohn is at the piano, hymnbook open. She hasn't been to church in a year of Sundays but the old, familiar hymns from her Baptist childhood back in Sanger, TX, sometimes help her creative juices flow.

Not this time, it seems. Marijohn and John have been humming, talking, playing for two hours without success. Maybe the well is dry for the day.

"'When the roll is called up yonder, when the roll . . .' John, I guess we've met our Waterloo. Shall we call it a day?" Marijohn closes her hymn book.

"Waterloo . . . Waterloo . . . ," her partner croons. Grabbing a guitar, he strikes up a chord.

Marijohn enters with a line: "Where will you meet your Waterloo?"

"John, that's a hit!"

"It's the corniest thing I ever heard."

"I don't care. It's a hit. Let's write it."

A verse from Napoleon. A stanza from the Bible. A bit of rhyme. A half-hour later, a million seller is on paper. For years Stonewall Jackson sings it on the Opry.

The golden years roll by. Marijohn's name appears on more hit songs. Performer Lefty Frizzell takes her *Long Black Veil* to the top. Old pal Red Foley makes hay with her *Travelin' Man*. Webb Pierce strikes fire with *Shanghaied*, written by Marijohn and Mel Tillis. Jimmie C. Newman brings her national recognition with *PT 109*. Singers flock to Marijohn as they seek new material to record. Her royalties mount. Her reputation rockets into the stratosphere.

She parties with the "beautiful people" in Nashville, New York, and Los Angeles. "You're the greatest, Marijohn, absolutely the greatest," they tell her. And, "Wherever do you get so many ideas for songs?"

Precious Memories

When the headiness wears off, sad nostalgia rolls in like chilling fog. Memories of her Texas childhood drift through her mind.

In her memory she catches the aroma of fresh Veribest Bread from her Melson family's bakery. She visualizes the Bible on Daddy Ernest's desk above the drawer where he kept his revolver. He never used the gun, but he opened the Bible hundreds of times to the Depression bums and hoboes who found him an easy touch.

Marijohn wipes away a tear and remembers how her "Daddyboy" would plunk her down on the piano stool and then, lifting his fiddle bow, would play along with her as she sang, *Jesus Loves Me*.

Then beloved Daddyboy was stricken with cancer. She had 11 years of straight A's behind her when his pain became so great that she had to make the bread deliveries. He never complained, but she could read the suffering in his eyes. She was his only child; how she hurt for him.

"Come closer, Daughter John," he whispered as he used his pet name for her. "Promise me you'll go to college so you won't have to be an ear player like me . . . Take care of your mother . . .." Then he was gone.

"Ernest Melson was a good man, like Bartholomew," the preacher intoned over his coffin. Marijohn hardly listened. The questions, the doubts, the whys flooded her mind. People all over Texas had been praying for her Daddyboy; he had died. What good was prayer, anyway?

A month later Marijohn graduated from high school with honors. Then she was off to Baylor University, where the music teacher pronounced, "Marijohn, you aren't a singer. Give up the idea." Another professor told her, "Stop singing danceband style." Never mind that she now had her own radio show. Country music wasn't approved of by her teachers.

She transferred to Hardin-Simmons University and became the first female member of the famous Hardin-Simmons Cowboy Band. One night during a parade in Dallas, a handsome man on a white horse rode up beside her and announced in a deep voice, "Howdy, I'm Tex Ritter."

Tex got her an audition for the movies. A producer offered a contract. "Thank you kindly," Marijohn said, "but I promised my daddy I would finish school." She had another reason: her sweetheart, football player Bedford Russell.

She and Bedford married right after graduation and during World War II. He joined the Army Air Force and got his wings and orders for North Africa. A year later the telegram arrived. Captain Russell had been taken prisoner and put on an Italian sub. British planes sunk the sub in the middle of the Mediterranean. His body could not be recovered.

Keeping the Dream Alive

Twenty-one and widowed, Marijohn took a job teaching music. She began drinking too much and remarried too soon. At 29 she was divorced and the mother of a young son, Bucky. She taught Bucky to sing, just as Daddyboy had taught her. She moved to Springfield, MO, where Ralph Foster, owner of Radio Station KWTO, for $25 a week hired Bucky to sing on Red Foley's Country Jubilee.

The only job Marijohn could get was singing in a piano bar. She felt guilty about promoting drinking when alcohol was destroying Red Foley, Hank Williams, and other great talents. But she kept telling herself, "Things will get better. It can't be much worse."

One night a lawyer heard her in the bar. "Hey, you ought to be in Nashville," he urged. "If you're going to shoot tigers, go where the tigers are."

With less than $100 in her pocket he packed up little Bucky and headed for Tennessee. She went to work in a piano bar called "The Voodoo" and kept the dream alive. One night an advertising executive drank himself under the table while he listened to her sing. Then he went out and almost killed himself in a wreck. Marijohn heard the news and felt terrible.

"God, help me break out of this," she moaned.

A week later she was working as a songwriter at Cedarwood Publishing for Jim Denny, one of the biggest writers in Country music. She was on her way up; God was only a memory.

The big hits occurred rapidly: *Make the Waterwheel Roll* with Mel Tillis; *Dying for Love*, recorded by Jimmie C.

Newman; and *Goodnight, Mama, Goodnight, Papa* by old friend Red Foley. Then her sponsor, Jim Denny, died from cancer.

Everything seemed so unfair. First her father, then Bedford, and now the publisher who had given her a chance. She was angry at God but would not admit it. She'd show Hin and the world. She got a partner and opened her own house— Buckhorn Publishing, named for Bucky.

Buckhorn was established when Country music was booming in Nashville. Branson was only a remote blip on a Missouri map. The fans were arriving at the Opry by the thousands to hear Roy Acuff, Red Foley, Patsy Cline, Kitty Wells, Loretta Lynn, Hawkshaw Hawkins, Cowboy Copas, Billy Walker, and the other stars. The performers and songwriters were like family to Marijohn. When one suffered, they all did.

Then the plane crash occurred that killed Hawkshaw, Patsy, Cowboy, and Cowboy's son-in-law, Randy Hughes. This was followed by the death of star Jack Anglin on his way to Patsy's funeral and the fatal mishap that took the lives of Jim Reeves and his road-manager and pianist, Dean Manuel.

Marijohn knew them all. She was numb with grief over the loss of so many friends. The fact that Bucky was making it by himself and didn't need his mother's tutelage any more didn't help. To her life seemed worthless.

"I Can't Even Kill Myself"

The rhymes and music wouldn't start up in her head. She began to hate songwriting. Tired and listless she became a recluse in a little house in the country.

Thanksgiving Day, 1964, Marijohn took all the pills and aspirin in the house and lay down to die. Red Foley and Mel Tillis showed up and brought her around.

"Marijohn, how many pills did you take?" Red shouted.

"D-d-don't you e-e-e-e-ver do this a-gain," stuttered Mel.

Mel and Red snapped her out of the depression. She made a tour to the Far East. Back home after New Year's, she felt the melancholy return.

Easter morning, about 5 a.m., she book her rifle, placed the butt on the floor, laid the end of the barrel along her neck, and squeezed the trigger. The bullet zinged past her ear and bounced harmlessly off the wall. It fell back on the floor. She tried again; again the bullet deflected.

Fingering a misshapen piece of lead she mumbled in a daze, "I can't even kill myself." Then she was struck by the thought that the God she had left in Texas must be trying to tell her something. As her eyes moistened, she let the tears flow. For the first time in years she cried.

Back at work she read a letter from an American soldier in Germany: "I'm a fellow Texan. Your cousin said I should look you up when I come to Nashville." It was signed "Captain Kris Kristofferson." She had never heard of him.

Marijohn always had been an easy mark for aspiring young musicians. Kris was different from most. He had class and polish; he had been a Rhodes Scholar and a helicopter pilot. He had even written short stories for the *Atlantic Monthly* and had been invited to teach at West Point. "I'm gonna make us both rich," he promised Marijohn.

She signed the clean-cut, scholarly youth to a Buckhorn contract and gave him a small advance to supplement the minimal wage he was getting as a janitor at nearby Columbia Records,

Kris and other young artists who looked up to Marijohn and other members of the Nashville establishment were themselves searching for meaning in life. Marijohn couldn't help them there, for she was still seeking herself. Lately into

Buddhism and fortune-telling, she was holding seances at her house.

She thought a long, leisurely voyage might help. En route to Rome she felt compelled to take a ship across the Mediterranean. She had the uncanny sense that she would know when the ship passed the spot where Bedford had gone down in the sub 20 years before.

At 11 o'clock on the second night out she began crying uncontrollably. She looked at a new friend she had met and sobbed, "This is it. This is where Bedford went down. I'm going up on deck."

As she and her friend emerged into the salty air, the wind suddenly died and the sea became as smooth as glass. She felt a sudden release, as if a tremendous load had been lifted. The hurt from Bedford's death was gone.

She spent a few days singing in Rome, enjoyed a week of rest with actor Dennis Weaver and his wife, Jerry, and journeyed to Israel to see the holy places that were familiar to her from Baptist Sunday-school days. Drawn along by an invisible force she felt herself on a pilgrimage bound for she knew not where.

Once Marijohn was back in Nashville, Kris Kristofferson was making it with *For the Good Times*, a property of Marijohn's publishing house. The bad news was that her partner in Buckhorn had terminal cancer.

Then her mother passed away. Next, her 83-year-old uncle became gravely ill. As the closest relative Marijohn felt duty-bound to care for him. Her publishing company floundered while she was away. She returned to face possible financial ruin.

She dismissed the thought of seeking counsel from a preacher. The ones she remembered pointed their fingers and preached hell-fire and damnation. She could see herself telling a pastor her story and hearing the stern voice say, "You made your bed. Now repent or lie in it." She couldn't take that.

Flipping through the Yellow Pages she found "Dial-a-Prayer" and called the number. A recorded voice assured, "God loves you. He cares." She called another number for an appointment.

When Marijohn emerged from her shiny, midnight-blue Cadillac, the young minister saw an attractive red-haired woman in lizard-skin boots and full-length mink coat worn over tailored shirt and blue jeans.

"How may I help you?" he asked.

"I guess I have every problem anybody can have, young man." At his request, she told him about the mess she was in.

"Well, why don't we just thank God for all this?" he said.

Marijohn stared at him in surprise. "I guess I never thought of that, but I'll try."

The preacher prayed. Then she got into her car and drove back to her house. She cried all the way and prayed over and over, "Thank You, Lord. I don't know why, but thank You. Thank You."

She never again saw the young minister who had helped her open the door to restored fellowship with the God of her childhood.

During the next few days she read her Bible and prayed, while a line kept running through her mind, "I have returned . . I have returned."

She knew a song was emerging and wrote:

I have returned to the God of my childhood,
To the same simple faith as a child I knew . . .

The words rushed like a torrent until she finished the song. Many problems remained unresolved. "How can I make it,

Lord?" The answer arrived, *Let me help you, one day at a time.* That was the secret; she started to put it in song.

After she muddled through a few lines, she asked Kris Kristofferson to help. working together they quickly completed what would become the most popular gospel song in history, *One Day at a Time.*

Marijohn has since written scores of other gospel songs. Some are sung on the Opry, on national television shows, and by performers in many languages around the world. She herself frequently has told on television how God brought her back to the faith of her childhood.

"It took a long time for God to deal with me," she says. "I had to go through a lot of deep water, but thank God, I've finally found what life is all about."

Jack Greene: "I Went for 40 Years without Going to Church"

In many ways the story of "country gentleman" Jack Greene parallels that of Marijohn Wilkins. At age 9 Jack began performing when his mother taught him to play the guitar. He learned such songs as *Froggy Went a-Courtin'* and *Letter Edged in Black.*

The Greenes lived in Maryville, a little town in the Smoky Mountains of East Tennessee. Jack heard Roy Acuff, Archie Campbell, Kitty Wells, and Eddie Arnold on radio station WGAP in Maryville. Those were his "teachers" while he was growing up. As a teen-ager Jack sang on WGAP and another station in nearby Knoxville.

Jack's parents were Christians. He attended church faithfully until he was 17 and went to Atlanta to "follow my dream", he says. "Then I kind of drifted away from the church. Saturday nights I worked late and didn't get up in time."

While he was performing in a nightclub, he met Jack Drake, the bass player for Ernest Tubb. "He found out I had been in the army," Jack Greene says, "and had training with diesel engines. He needed me to work on their bus."

For five years Jack worked with Ernest Tubb and the Texas Troubadours. He became known as "The Singing Drummer." Finally Ernest told Jack to "go out" on his own and "pay for your kids' education. If you can't make it, you can always come back and be one of my Troubadours."

The rest, you might say, is history. Jack became a regular performer on the Grande Ole Opry. From 1961 to 1992 he recorded more than 30 albums plus five more with Jeannie Seely, with whom he sang as a duet for 11 years. In 1967 he won an unprecedented four Country Music Association awards: "Song of the Year" with There Goes My Everything, "Album of the Year", "Singer of the Year", and "Male Vocalist of the Year." Only three other persons have attained this achievement in 25 years of CMA awards.

After he left home, Jack married and fathered five children, who gave him six grandchildren. "When they were growing up, I was gone constantly with [Ernest] Tubbs," he laments. "We were doing 300 days a year. For a period of 19 years I was never home." None of his children or six grandchildren has entered show business.

Divorced from his first wife, Jack remarried in 1980. Eight years later Billy Walker and his wife happened to invite the Greenes to a Christmas get-together with a number of Christians. "God began to work on their hearts," Billy remembers. "Jack and June accepted the Lord. They dressed in tuxedos to be baptized at Hickory Heights Baptist Church in Hendersonville."

"I went for 40 years without going to church," Jack told writer Dolores Cole. "I didn't ever even give it a thought. But

I never forgot the two things Mama instilled in me growing up; you're known by the company you keep and don't get above your raisings."

Jack is now a deacon in the Hickory Heights Church, which is also attended by numerous other Opry performers, including Bill Monroe, Ferlin Husky, and Cal Smith.

Bobby Wood: "They Rolled Me Out of the Operating Room 'Dead'"

Bobby Wood is another old-timer who has returned to his roots. Bobby started singing with his family in Baptist churches back in Mississippi and then moved to Memphis, where he worked with Elvis Presley, Jerry Lee Lewis, and B.J. Thomas.

"Back then I suspected Elvis was on medication and heavy," Bobby recalls. "B.J. Thomas was in worse shape. He had taken so many uppers and downers that he got to be like an 80-year-old man. I'd always point him to the Lord. He knew that was where I was coming from, even when I wasn't walking with the Lord at that time. Later B.J. got his life straightened out. He's serving the Lord today."

When Bobby moved to Nashville, he got a couple of records out that did well. *If I'm a Fool* climbed to number one in the charts. He also wrote songs. Crystal Gayle, Loretta Lynn's little sister, hit with *You've Been Talkin' in Your Sleep*, written by Bobby Wood and Roger Crook.

"I thought I had life made and the world by the tail," Bobby says. "Then the Lord straightened me out."

Things happened this way:

Bobby and five other musicians left Nashville in a station wagon to perform in Ohio. About 5 a.m. the wagon had a headon crash with a semi. The trucker died in the wreck; the musicians went to the hospital in an ambulance.

"They rolled me out of the operating room 'dead'," Bobby says. "They left me in the corridor for an orderly to take to the morgue. A black doctor happened to walk by and saw my arm flop out from under the sheet. Normally he would have just put the arm bak, but something told him to feel for a pulse. He felt a faint beat. The doctors went back to work. When I came around, that black physician told me, 'Young man, if you don't believe in God now, there's no hope for you.'"

Afterward Bobby met a girl named Janice in a recording studio. After they were married and at a time when Bobby was trying to get off drugs, Bobby went for counseling at the Lord's Chapel. "They prayed for me to receive the Holy Spirit. I didn't sense any great change until somebody offered me a joint two weeks later. I turned it down just like that. Next it was booze. I turned that down. Then it was a toot of cocaine and I said *no* without even thinking about it. When I realized what I'd done, I knew it had to be the Lord. I hadn't been able to do that by myself."

Bobby and Janice became involved in a Friday-night Bible study and intercessory prayer group. "We have a long prayer list," Bobby notes. "I don't know how many people we've marked off as having met the Lord. One who was recently saved in our house is the wife of a top songwriter in town."

In the music world Bobby concentrated on songwriting and recording sessions. Known as one of the best studio artists in Nashville he works with George Jones, Loretta Lynn, and other established stars.

One night he "got a chance to witness to Loretta. She wanted to read my palms. I said, 'No thank you, Loretta. I don't believe in that stuff.'

She asked, 'Why don't you?'

"I'm a Christian,' I told her.

"Well, I used to be a member of the Church of Christ. I

was raised that way and got baptized", she replied.

"I said, 'I used to be a Baptist, but now I'm a Christian.'

"Loretta knows that it isn't a denomination or a religion. It's God and you. I think most people like her want to believe."

Vic Willis: "We're Just Getting Closer to One Another and to the Lord"

Vic Willis has been around longer than Bobby Wood. Born one of six sons to a fiddling coal miner, Vic grew up in Oklahoma. Her was baptized a Mormon and later became an Episcopalian. With two brothers, Guy and Skeeter, Vic formed the "Oklahoma Wranglers" trio.

World War II landed Vic on Normandy beach on "D-Day." He and three buddies were hit by an artillery shell. His friends were killed on the spot; Vic was seriously hurt with a thigh wound. He prayed, "Lord, if you'll get me out of this, I'll be the best person who ever lived. I'll do anything you want." However, when the shooting stopped, he went right on cursing and telling dirty jokes.

After the war, the Oklahoma Wranglers became the Willis Brothers. They joined the Grand Ole Opry, then left to help Eddie Arnold with his network radio and stage show. Then they became the first group to sing backup for Hank Williams, as well as the first featured act on the Jubilee USA show in Springfield, MO. Later they gave a premiere performance as the first Country entertainers to sing in Washington DC's Constitution Hall. In 1960 they rejoined the Opry.

Over a span of three decades the Willis Brothers appeared on more than 1,500 television shows, sold millions of records, and toured the world. With Guy emceeing and playing the guitar, Skeeter as the "smilin' fiddler", and Vic doubling as accor-

192

dionist and pianist, they became one of the top Country and Western acts of modern times. Vic also developed a successful jingle business—writing rhymes for radio and television commercials for Ford, General Motors, Kelloggs, and other clients.

Despite his success, however, Vic was no stranger to sorrow. In the mid-'50s he lost his father to black lung disease. In 1960 his mother succumbed to cancer. Vic's fellow performer and brother Skeeter Willis died in 1976. Shortly after Skeeter's death brothers Joe and Guy were diagnosed as having terminal cancer. Vic's other brother then became critically ill with emphysema.

Vic rebuilt the trio with C.W. Mitchell and Curtis Young. when C.W. was out for a while with a broken back, Vic joked on the Opry, "Just call us the Blue Cross boys."

One of the best-liked performers in Nashville, Vic was elected executive director of the Association of Country Entertainers. Around this time Vic's own life began falling apart.

Under the impossible load of being performer, executive director of ACE, husband to wife Joyce and father to twin daughters, besides visiting his hospitalized brothers, Vic developed an ulcer. When it began hemorrhaging, his doctor put him in the hospital.

Though the rest was helpful, Vic soon fell into a deep depression. For the first time he began having serious marital problems. "I wasn't thinking clearly. It got to the point that I didn't like the entertainers or hardly anyone. Day after day I would go to my office, take the phone off the hook, and refuse to answer the door or my mail.

"During this time I became involved with another woman. I finally had to admit this to my wife. She sued for divorce, which she should have done. Joe and Guy died, leaving me with only one brother who was still very sick. I had a complete breakdown and was admitted to a psychiatric ward.

"A Catholic priest and an Episcopal priest tried to help me. The psychiatrist said I had suppressed everything—the grief over my brothers' deaths and the turmoil over my divorce.

"Through all of this my former wife, my daughters, and my friends at the Opry stood behind me. When I got out of the hospital, my former wife felt we couldn't go back together, but she said we could continue to be good friends.

"Still in a deep depression I blamed myself for everything. I prayed for forgiveness, but I couldn't forgive myself.

"I started thinking of ways to commit suicide. A friend asked me if I had nerve enough to go through with it. I said, 'I fought at Normandy. I saw men shot in half. I was wounded and survived. That ought tell you something.

"'Maybe', I told him, 'I'll ram my car into a bridge abutment. I could jump in the river, take a parachute lesson and forget to pull the cord, or take a '38 and blow my brains out. That'd be real quick.'"

Long suspicious and critical of entertainers who talked about the Bible and salvation, he resented people telling him, "God bless you." He thought they were hypocrites and said so when they were out of earshot.

The board of directors of ACE asked him to continue as executive director. Moved by this show of support Vic began seeing his colleagues in a different light. One day during an ACE board meeting at which Hank Snow, Barbara Mandrell, Roy Acuff, and Connie Smith were present, he said, "During the past few months I've learned a lot about you, my fellow entertainers—a lot that I didn't know before. I've grown to love, respect, and appreciate you for your goodness."

He looked directly at Connie Smith. "I'm sorry that I've been sarcastic and critical behind your back, Connie. I've come to believe that you're a good Christian girl. I love all of you." He said down in tears.

When the depression lingered, Vic's former wife asked him to consider spiritual help. When Vic agreed, she suggested calling Connie Smith's pastor, Billy Ray Moore. "You've told me a number of times that she's a real Christian. I'll set up an appointment for you," she offered.

That was December 1, 1979. Mrs. Willis made the appointment and Vic, looking 10 years older than his 58 years, drove over to the Lord's Chapel.

"I bared my soul to Connie's preacher," he says. "I told him everything.

"He said, 'Vic, you've got all this guilt. You've asked God to forgive you, and He has. Everybody else but you has forgiven you. Now why would you ask God to forgive you when you won't forgive yourself?'

"It took weeks for that to sink in. I felt like the awfulest person in the whole world. Brother Moore kept assuring me, 'God erased that. It's erased, gone, no more. Accept God's Word that He's forgiven you.

"I went to the service and saw 1,300 people praising the Lord in song. People would walk up and put their arms around my neck and say, 'I love you.' Some didn't even know who I was.

"I was flooded with love. Overwhelmed, I told my neighbor Clarence, 'You've gotta go over there to the Lord's Chapel with me.'

"He said, 'What do you like about it so much?'

"I said, 'They love you. They really do. They come up and grab you and say, "I love you, brother." If you want to sing, it's OK. If not, don't sing. You hear people that can't sing very good; then you hear somebody like Connie Smith with a beautiful voice come out above everybody. She's sitting there by her fine husband, her lap full of kids. You're listening. She starts clapping her hands and then looks up at you and smiles. Others are clapping and smiling. It's wonderful.'

"'Clarence,' I kept on, 'you see people with long hair, beards, blacks, whites, young people, all kinds. They're carrying Bibles. They know Christ. They know what love is. They hug you, a complete stranger, and say they love you.'"

Vic sees the world around him changing for the better. "Being a Christian is a wonderful thing. I see more and more people coming to the Lord.

"We've always helped one another when we were sick by sending flowers and visiting at the hospital. Now a lot of us send Scripture verses we think are suited to a person's need. Sometimes we get together and pray in a dressing room. It isn't a preachy thing. We're just getting closer to each other and to the Lord."

Vic's spiritual experience rejuvenated his musical career as well. He reconstituted the Vic Willis Trio. He began doing old songs which he and his departed brothers loved. These included *Cimarron, Sioux City Sue*, and *Just a Closer Walk with Thee*. Besides his membership on the Opry, he was elected secretary/treasurer of Local 57 of the American Federation of Musicians on Music Row. This and his continued involvement with ACE are testimonials top the high regard with which the "new" Vic Willis is held by fellow entertainers.

Glen Campbell: "I've Never Been So Happy"

You think "Rhinestone Cowboy" when you hear Glen Campbell. "Prodigal" is perhaps the better name for the former cotton-picker and garbage-truck driver, who climbed to the heights of stardom and fell to the depths of personal misery before he returned to the God of his childhood.

Glen Campbell was born April 22, 1936, one of 12 children in Billstown, AR, population 450. His father was a poor country Baptist preacher who couldn't earn enough from the pulpit to support his large family. So the Campbells picked cotton to keep food on the table and clothes on their backs.

"We had no choice but to go to church," Glen says, as he remembers the preaching, singing, and Bible-reading on which he was reared. "I never got away [from Jesus]. I just wasn't close to Him. I always had a sense of responsibility about my faith, but something always got in the way of it. Sin has a way of doing that."

Glen's best-remembered Bible verse was Matthew 5:17, where Jesus said, *"I have not come to destroy the law but to fulfill it."*

"I knew," he says, "that Jesus was the Way."

Like many other Country boys he listened to the Opry and other shows on the radio and dreamed of a career in Country music. At 14 he quit school to join an uncle's touring band. At 22 he moved to Los Angeles and worked as a studio musician. At 29 he joined the Beach Boys for a short period before he went solo and hit it big with two crossover songs, *Gentle on My Mind* and *By the Time I Get to Phoenix*. At age 32 he was the top-selling recording artist in America. He won four Grammies and the title "Country Music Entertainer of the Year." He was featured in his own television variety show and starred with John Wayne in the movie, "True Grit."

His first marriage failed. His second marriage, to beautician Billie Jean Nunley, lasted 16 years. His third marriage, to the former wife of his friend Mac Davis, lasted only four years. For the next year and a half he was linked to singing sensation Tanya Tucker, young enough to be his daughter. Their relationship made headlines in gossip tabloids. Glen called her the "real true love of my life." When their alleged affair was over, Tanya lamented, "I guess I got too old for him.

You're talking about a man twice my age, who's had three marriages and five kids, who's been very successful but still has this insecurity."

In 1982 Glen married his fourth wife, Kim. Glen met her when she was a professional dancer in New York City. His heart was "softening toward God" when they were introduced. He recalls praying before the meal on their first date. They were married October 25, 1981. After committing themselves to Christ, they were baptized by Glen's minister brother on December 22 in a cold creek in Arkansas.

At this time Glen and Kim were living in Phoenix and attending North Phoenix Baptist Church. Pastor Richard Jackson took a special interest in Glen and encouraged him to move forward in the Christian life. Glen was delivered from drugs—instantly, he says. Alcohol took a little longer. "I finally said, 'Lord, I want out of this.' With Jesus, if you ask for it, you get it. 'Ask, and you shall receive, seek and you shall find.'"

Glen and Kim now have three children of their own: Cal, 9; Shannon, 7; and Ashley, 5. The two older children already have accepted Christ, Glen says. Two of his children from previous marriages reportedly also have become Christians as a result of the change seen in their father's life.

The former Rhinestone Cowboy now is winning awards for gospel music. In 1986 he won the Dove award for "Best Gospel Recording by a Secular Artist." The song: *No More Night.* A second Glen Campbell song, *Where Shadows Never Fall,* recently won a Dove award as "Best Southern Gospel recorded Song of the Year."

Glen appeared in some 70 shows at the Grand Palace during the 1992 season in Branson. Supporting performers included many of the biggest names in the country field: the Statler Brothers, the Oak Ridge Boys, Sawyer Brown, Ronnie

Millsap, Waylon Jennings, Marie Osmond, and the Smothers Brothers. Glen's repertoire ranges from secular to gospel. He keeps working for ways to "fit in" his testimony and more Christian music into his shows.

Without Christ he'd "probably be wallowing in hell right now. I've never been so happy," he recently told writer Teresa Shields Parker, "and so content with who Glen Campbell is as I am right now. It's because Jesus Christ is living through me."

Chapter 12
Country Music Comin' Home

Jimmie Rodgers' first royalty check amounted to all of $27. Roy Acuff didn't get his first $100 in gate receipts until 1940. Roy is a multi-millionaire now with a 16-foot-by-8-foot, silver-gray, Georgian-marble gravestone already in place.

Rags-to-riches stories are all over the Country scene. As a child Dolly Parton wore rags and remnants and was reared in a house with "four rooms and a path." She now has her own theme park, performs in Las Vegas for more than $350,000 a week, and rakes in millions from record royalties.

Country entertainers "making it" are in "tall cotton". So are the record companies of which no less than 238 in Music City. Nashville remains the Recording Capital of the World.

Statler Brothers: "Whatever Happened to Randolph Scott?"

Country music always has changed with the times. The big cultural revolution began in the late 1960s when Chicago music critic Gary Deeb observed: "For sheer sensuality and overt appeal to sexual interests, there's nothing more racy on the air" than Country lyrics.

Said Paul Harvey: "Historically Country music reflected apple-pie patriotism, virtue, boy-girl romance. Much of today's pottage is downright porno."

A sample of '70s songs suggests that Deeb and Harvey were on target. *You Lift Me Up to Heaven When You Lay Me Down,* sang Reba McIntire. *How Far Do You Want to Go?* asked Ronnie McDowell. Roy Clark didn't want a "piece of paper"—just for his girl to love him for "love's own sake." Dolly Parton compared her body to a *Bargain Store.* Jack Greene and Jeannie Seely (with deep, plunging neckline) sang, "My love is yours for the taking, so take me . . .." Marty Robbins, with his shirt unbuttoned almost to his belt buckle, had "day dreams about night things in the middle of the afternoon." Glen Campbell crooned, "When you're lying next to me, just love me every which way you can"—about an affair between two people not married to each other. Other titles include: *Let's Get It While the Gittin's Good* and *She Was Wild and She Was Willing.*

You could sum up the lyrics in one word: SEX—almost always the kind once considered wrong but which had become a badge of honor. As Don Williams, a believer in love, observed: "I don't believe virginity is as common as it used to be."

The Statler Brothers asked, "Whatever happened to Randolph Scott" and to the old cowboy movies in which honor and justice always prevailed? Whatever happened to the sweet and bittersweet Country love ballads which stopped short of the bedroom door? What happened to those songs in which the sinner always paid a price for following the siren's call of infidelity?

Of course the old-timers—Roy Acuff, Billy Grammer, Stu Phillips, Hank Snow, and many others—still sang the old songs on the Opry. But it was the sexy stuff that got the airplay on the big stations.

The honky-tonk, cheating era began around 1950. Jimmie Wakely and Margaret Whiting cropped up with *One Has My*

Name—The Other Has My Heart and *Slipping Around.* In *Back Street Affair* Webb Pierce made adultery appear honorable.

The big tidal wave of promiscuity that swept through the industry in the late 1960s and early 1970s influenced many of the biggest stars. Loretta Lynn had a stack of hits about illicit sex. They included *Another Man Loved Me Last Night* about a woman cheating on her man who'd been cheating on her and *The Pill* about the new freedom that allowed a woman to enjoy illicit sex without fear of getting pregnant. A few stations, mostly in the South, refused to play these and other records with similar themes. Some preachers cited them as evidence that Country music was bent on destroying families. Arthur Smith, one of the few big song publishers who continued to champion traditional values, warned: "What the songs of today say influences the country more than the laws. Music is that important. It influences our youth," Smith declared. Social scientists, meanwhile, were counting record numbers of out-of-wedlock babies. Kitty Wells observed, "If a woman had sung songs like Loretta's 20 years ago, she'd have been taken out and tarred and feathered."

Loretta maintained that her personal life was one thing and her music another. In 25 years of marriage, "I ain't never cheated on [my husband] Doo," she says. Soap operas, not Country music, were the ruination of America.

Concern arose that Country music was losing its instrumental simplicity. Some of the older performers didn't care for the drums and cymbals that once had been banned from the Opry. Roy Acuff had "nothing against drums" but said he could "beat a rhythm on a number two tomato can. Rhythm is the basic element of music, but it shouldn't drown out the sweetness of the melody."

The purists disliked Country singers doing pop and pop

singers meddling with Country. Let the two remain separate, they said. But the crossovers and mixing continued. Deciding whether a song was Country or pop was often difficult to say. Many were both, not to consider the invasion of rock.

Grandpa Jones: "When Rock and Roll Came In, I Went Out"

What really rankled traditional performers such as Grandpa Jones, Billy Grammer, and Stu Phillips were the questionable lyrics.

Said Grandpa: "Too many writers are turning out skin songs and not the gentle, down-to-earth music. When rock and roll came in, I went out."

Billy Grammer told Nashville reporter Bill Hance about his run-in with a Miami deejay who refused to play Billy's new record, *Family Man*: "The deejay said if my song had more sex, it would sell and he would play it. I got kinda mad."

Still steaming when his next turn arrived to perform on the Opry, Billy told the audience. "Country music is becoming a smutty word. It doesn't need to be this way. I don't like it. For a Country song to be popular these days, it has to have lyrics about lying in bed with someone and getting them pregnant before they got married."

When Billy stopped, a moment's stony silence could be heard; then the crowd erupted into a thunderous ovation. The national wire services picked up Billy's remarks. Newspapers quoted him across the country. The skittish Opry management told Billy to remember that he had a captive audience. Billy promised to "refrain in the future."

Still, Billy said, "we've got to speak up somehow. Somebody has got to put down some guidelines. I wish the Opry would I know they're concerned.

"Some in our industry will tell you people want the sex and the four-letter words. One star told me that this was the 'in thing.' I don't agree."

Ricky Skaggs Believes Music Should Mean Something

Today, 12 years later, the Country-music scene is more encouraging. "Today's Country music has values," declares Billy Walker. "[Vice President] Dan Quayle was right. It's TV and entertainment out of Los Angeles and New York that's dirty and rotten and no good."

Billy Walker cites Ricky Skaggs as a leader of the new wave of artists who are standing up for family and traditional values. "Ricky's been at the Opry eight or nine years. He enjoys reading his Bible. He's not a golden oldie like some of us."

Billy Walker and Ricky Skaggs may be a generation apart, but they share the same faith and moral values. "Ricky," says *Country Music* magazine columnist Bob Allen, "is one of those popular artists who's never quite let go of the noble . . . notion that one's music should mean something: that it should enlighten listeners, or at least strive for some higher purpose or subtle spiritual awakening beyond mere entertainment and sentimentality."

Ricky champions more than the lyrics of traditional values.

Some say that, more than anybody else, he helped "save" Country music in the 1980s from becoming smashed on the "rocks" of wild rock and dissolute living. "Ricky really led this whole new wave of music," says fiddler Mark O'Connor. "He's the elder statesman of the new bunch of artists."

Ricky doesn't take all the credit but says, "The Lord is using Country music to speak morals, wisdom, truth, and righteous lifestyle to people."

Here's Ricky on stage at the Grand Ole Opry declaring "I love bluegrass. I want to keep the traditional music alive." The fans are pushing up to the front to take pictures. Ricky waves at a familiar face. "It's good to see you all tonight", he says and launches into *It's That Same Old Love*. The crowd hollers and applauds.

"Thank you very much It's that same old Grand Ole Opry that's been going for over 60 years." Ricky doesn't mention that he's the youngest performer ever to be invited to join the Opry.

In green sportscoat and plain button-down, dark shirt Ricky repeats, "It's good to see all of you tonight. Shout out where you're from!" A jumble of names of states and towns bounce back at the friendly redhead on stage.

Ricky holds a fiddle as he "makes welcome" the White Family, to which his wife, Sharon, belongs. Their music is sweet and soothing to the ear: "Deep within my heart lies a melody, a song of old San Antone . . .."

Ricky introduces his friend Justin Tubb, who sings, "I am still loving you, after all you put me through . . .." After a commercial break Ricky springs back on stage. He is bouncing, smiling, singing, "I'm a tellin' everyone you're at the top of my list." Suddenly he grabs Sharon and swings her around the stage in a dancing embrace. The crowd loves it.

No crying in your beer. No shack-up, one-night stand for Ricky, who reminds music lovers, *Life's Too Long (to Live Like This)* and *You Can't Take It With You When You Go.* "Just proud to be a Country boy." Ricky's heart is "to put out good messages and songs—family values and Christian values of marriage and love and hope for the future of families and children . . .."

Things were not always this way for Ricky, who knows firsthand the agony of family conflict and the pain of divorce when he was younger and much less committed to the values he sings about today. He's tried to learn from failure in his first marriage and has been working diligently for 11 years to build an enduring relationship with Sharon.

Ricky and Sharon live in Nashville with their two children–Molly, 8, and Lucas, 3. Ricky's two children from his previous marriage— 14-year-old Mandy and 13-year-old Andrew—live with them for part of the year.

Both Ricky and Sharon are on the road a lot—Sharon with her family and Ricky with his band. "We fight for time together at home," Ricky says, "and plan schedules to accommodate each other as much as possible."

"Sometimes when he's on the road and I'm here," Sharon told *Charisma* magazine, "the only time we can talk is on the phone in the middle of the night, but we do it. We've learned that if we don't keep that, this thing doesn't work very well."

"We really work on our marriage," Ricky told writer Dick Brunson. "We pray together. We put our kids to bed together and read to them. We shut the TV off an hour before bedtime and spend times with the kids in the Word. We lay our hands on them and bless then and pray for them."

Ricky also helps Sharon around the house when he is home. "I clean the kitchen. sometimes I cook. I change Luke's diapers. I take him so she can read the Bible and pray . . . True masculinity is an inward brokenness and a desire for more of God in our life."

On the road Ricky and members of his band try to attend church in the town in which they're performing. When he is home, he and Sharon take the children to Abundant Life Church, a nondenominational congregation in a suburb of Nashville. Sharon helps teach a Sunday-school class there.

They also maintain close friendships with several fellow entertainers. Sharon calls her friend Barbara Fairchild "my spiritual mama."

During one meeting with Barbara and her husband, Milton Carroll, the talk swung to corruption in the music industry. Barbara suggested, "We need to pray about this."

Within a few weeks Barbara, Sharon, and Sharon's sitter, Cheryl White, were meeting regularly in the Skaggs' home to pray for Country-music people. The prayer group attracted so many people that it was moved to Music Row in Nashville. After three years it's still going, with more than 100 people meeting every Tuesday to pray for an awakening to morality and family concerns in the Country-music industry.

Forever and Ever, Amen

One of their continuing prayer concerns is that God will raise up more Christian songwriters. An answer to that prayer occurred when Paul Overstreet's *Forever and Ever, Amen* was recorded by Randy Travis and became a top hit. Named "Single of the Year" in 1986 by the Country Music Association, the anthem to faithfulness in marriage struck a new chord with millions of fans.

Paul Overstreet's story is not a new one. Son of a Baptist minister and aspiring to the big time, he arrived in Nashville after he finished high school in Newton, MS. Hit by one rejection after another and with no money for rent, he slept wherever he could find shelter.

In 1983 George Jones sent Paul's *Same Old Me* soaring into the Top Ten. Sad to say, Paul admits, "I blew all my money on wine, women, and song."

When this lifestyle didn't bring happiness, Paul turned his "life back over to the Lord." He bought a modern version of the Bible and began reading. "I was so convicted that I could only stand to read a page at a time. Many things in my life were abominations to the Lord," he recalled later for Nashville writer Marsha Gallardo. Finally he "told the Lord that if I couldn't live my life in a godly manner and be in the music business, then I just wouldn't be in it at all."

The next year, 1985, he was invited to sing on a Nashville show. A beautiful woman named Julie was the makeup artist. Three months later they were married. Paul, Julie, and their four children now live on an 82-acre farm a half-hour west of Nashville.

Paul's vow to live in a "godly manner" was fulfilled in a line of songs that is helping bring Country music back to moral basics. Songs like *Forever and Ever, Amen; Seein' My Father in Me; Love Can Build a Bridge; On the Other Hand; Battle Hymn of Love; Diggin' Up Bones;* and *Heroes.* These are songs that continue to be sung by some of the biggest stars of the 1980s, including Randy Travis and Pam Tillis.

For four years running Paul Overstreet has won BMI's "Songwriter of the Years" award. When Paul speaks, people in the industry listen.

"I try to stay away from 'woe, woe, pitiful me' type of songs," he told *Country America* magazine. "I don't want to write about falling out of love. I would rather write about falling deeper in love or getting deeper in a relationship with my wife or with my children. If I can share that with people and give them encouragement, I know it's going to enhance their lives."

Every Overstreet song is a story; he's heard some rewarding testimonials. One man told of how he had failed his wife and was sitting in his car, drinking beer and trying to get up courage to commit suicide. The radio was on. He heard Paul singing,

Daddy's come around to Mama's way of thinking,
No more staying out all night drinking . . .
He finally figured out he's got something worth
keeping . . .

The depressed husband repeated aloud the words *something worth keeping*. He unloaded the gun, pitched the beer cans out the window, and drove home to be reconciled with his wife.

"I've learned that God can use us in any business we're in," Paul told *Country America.* "I [once] thought if I were a Christian, I'd have to give up everything fun. But I learned differently. It's fun when you start doing things you don't regret."

Ricky Skaggs and Paul Overstreet have played big roles in the "coming home" of Country music. They and others with kindred spirits have demonstrated that good, wholesome, uplifting music is what Country-music fans want.

Make Way for Branson

The Branson "phenomenon" has taken the industry by storm. Branson, which transplanted performer Mel Tillis calls "a cross between Mayberry and Vegas", is raising corporate eyebrows in executive suites all across the country. Branson is getting special attention in Nashville, where disdainful industry insiders refer to it as "that other place."

With a resident population of only 3,706, Branson spells money in the sum of $1.5 billion left behind by five-million tourists in 1991. That's almost as much as visitors to the Opry, Opryland, and all other attractions spent in Nashville (population 514,000) last year.

Why is Branson bidding to replace Nashville as the

Country-music capital of the world? Mel Tillis cites one reason: "You go to Nashville you see the stars' homes. You come to Branson; you see the stars who come out to mingle with the fans after every show."

Branson is also set in a developer's dream country of forested mountains and valleys, clear streams, refreshing lakes, and friendly people.

But the biggest reason, just about everybody agrees, is clean entertainment. Branson proves that G-rated music—the kind the tickles Grandpa's funnybone without making Grandma blush—sells better than does R-rated smut and X-rated porno.

"Family entertainment sells," glows Missouri governor John Ashcroft, a Country-gospel singer himself. "And in Branson, it sells big."

Branson, named for the first postmaster of the town, is the almost smack-dab center of the southern Missouri Ozarks. For many years it was regarded as just a "poke and plumb town"—by the time you poke your hand out your car window to wave at somebody, you're plumb out of town. As a boy in northern Arkansas I passed through Branson on every trip to our big market town—Springfield, MO. Back then I had no idea that little Branson one day would become world-famous. All the Missouri action back in the '30s was then in Springfield.

Ralph Foster's Ozark Jubilee, originating in Springfield, was getting high ratings on network TV. Billy Walker was one of a number of performers engaged by Foster to go there and perform. "Ralph promised me $100 a show if I would come. When I got there, he cut it to $25." Billy, Red Foley, and numerous other Springfield entertainers soon moved on to Nashville and the Opry.

Shepherd of the Hills

The foundation for tourism in the Branson area was laid by Harold Bell Wright's Christian novel, *Shepherd of the Hills.* Published in 1907 the story is set at Inspiration Point, the second-highest spot in Missouri. It's just off Highway 76 west of Branson. Wright spun a semi-autobiographical tale about a discouraged city preacher who went to the Ozarks and became involved with a folksy family. After a while Wright discovered that the family was related to the past he was trying to forget. The story included a mysterious, masked band of outlaws called the Baldknobbers, with a few ghosts and a panther playing dead thrown in for interest. Panned by big-city critics, *Shepherd of the Hills* became one of the best-selling books in American history. It was so popular that readers began traveling to the Ozarks to meet the mountain people in the story.

The Pioneering Baldknobbers

The first music show in Branson featured four brothers—Bill, Bob, Lyle, and Jim Mabe, who grew up singing for their preacher father in churches and at funerals. The Mabes did their first performance in a hall over the police department that seated 50 people. While the brothers warmed up, their wives walked around town in country dresses carrying signs advertising the show. They used old-time homemade instruments, a washboard for rhythm, and a washtub bass and a dobro. They sang such crowd-pleasing favorites as *How Much Is that Doggie in the Window?* and *She'll Be Comin' Around the Mountain.* For future Friday- and Saturday-night performances they set a minimum gate of 15 people. "There were times," Bill Mabe recalls, "when we'd count noses and say, 'Sorry, folks, there won't be a show tonight.'"

By 1958 so many tourists were traveling to Branson that the Shepherd of the Hills Outdoor Theater was established to re-enact Wright's story in a pageant. The Mabe brothers played characters in the book and performed in the band. The Baldknobbers became the name of their pioneering comedy and music act.

When their show became too crowded, the Baldknobbers moved to the town skating rink, which accommodated 600 seats. In 1967 the singing Presleys opened the first theater on 76 Country Boulevard which became known as "The Strip." A year later the Baldknobbers built their own theater on "The Strip." The theater seats 1,700 people today.

The Baldknobbers still sing some of the old numbers of 30-years ago. Second and third Mabe generations now are performing. Commenting on the mega-growth, Bill Mabe says, "I never thought it would come to this."

The Branson Secret

The Baldknobbers is just one of two-dozen Country-music theaters which are filled every evening—spring, summer, and fall, with some featuring matinee shows. The fans love the entertainment. No one has need of a backstage pass. The stars mingle after every show. Says Mel Tillis, whose theater is off the Strip and on U.S. Highway 65 moving into Branson: "I'm a Country boy. This is like coming home. And there's good fishing here." Notes Roy Clark, who also has a showplace: "You don't have to worry about getting mugged outside." Boxcar Willie echoes the satisfaction of many tour-weary performers: "It gets me off the road."

The traffic's bad, but the food, lodging, and tickets are cheap compared to the big cities. Many fans arrive in church-tour groups. Seventy-one-year-old Glenn Johnson, who arrived with 44 other seniors in a Methodist church group from Texas, told *People* magazine, "We love it because of the good, clean, wholesome family atmosphere." Jack Herschend, president of the nearby Silver Dollar City theme park, told *Time*: "This is such a family place that anyone who tried to capture the off-color niche wouldn't work." To illustrate, Henry Mancini, guesting at Andy Williams' theater, made a stage comment that Williams had really "put his a__ on the line" by building a theater in Branson. Williams quickly reprimanded his guest: "We don't say a__ in Branson." The audience responded with thunderous applause. Says *People* magazine: "Sorry, Nashville," but Branson's "'the new world capital of Country music.'" Pioneer Bill Mabe puts the scene in better perspective: "There's more live Country music on the Branson Strip than anywhere else in the world. But Nashville is the recording place; I'll tell anybody that. I don't think Branson will ever be a recording center. Better to say that Branson is the world's top performing place, while Nashville remains the unquestioned recording center."

Whatever, Branson was one of three entertainment centers from which the 1992 Muscular Dystrophy Telethon originated. The other two were New York and Los Angeles.

Meanwhile, Back in Nashville

Billy Walker is one who is staying with the Opry in Nashville. "Branson's a beautiful place. I thought of moving there once. I could have done what Mel Tillis did, but when you have a lot of interests in one area, you can't just pick up and leave."

Nashville's Jimmie Snow doesn't "see little Branson with its traffic nightmare ever becoming the recording center of the world. I don't think Branson's going to mean that much to

213

Nashville because Nashville's not built like Branson. It wa
never geared to be like Branson. However, if they don't do
some things here, this town's going to be hurt—maybe in
tourists.

"Something else," continues Jimmie. The majority of the
performers are not your big stars of this moment. Garth
Brooks, Travis Tritt, and Billy Ray Cyrus, to mention three,
don't have places in Branson. Many of the guys in Branson
don't have record contracts anymore. They're not over the hill,
but they've made their money. They're looking for something
to do where they don't have to travel so much.

"So you're talking about two different things and two different types of people."

Does Jimmie see a revival of values and family commitments in Country music? "That's probably true. Maybe more
in Branson than in Nashville. Branson is appealing to my age
group—filling then up with family ideas.

"It isn't just Branson versus Nashville," Jimmie continues.
"It's generations in Country music. A lot of the oldtimers will
complain that [the new kind of Country music] is going to the
dogs. Well, I'm not particularly crazy about some of the new
Country music. But it's changing.

"I watched the TV talk shows when [Billy Ray] Cyrus hit
number one with *Achy, Breaky Heart*. They were all discussing
Branson and Nashville. They're appealing more to the young
here. But these young guys will grow up and become more
like the older ones.

"I'm just saying that this is what I'm seeing."

Jimmie hasn't "left the ministry", but he's no longer a pastor. "It got to where I was doing too much: Grand Ole Gospel
time, which we've been doing at the close of the Opry for 21
years, the church, and a studio with pews, which we called the
Carpenter's Shop, built next door to the church. I had to turn

loose of something. I felt I had done all I could accomplish as a pastor. I told the people I would be coming over to the studio. It wouldn't be quite the same as the church. We wouldn't have the Sunday school and the social activities. I'd still preach to them every Sunday morning and night and lead a mid-week Bible study. We'd be be videotaping this for a future cable TV outreach. Some members did go on to other churches. About 160 stayed and we've trained most of these to work in the studio.

"To pay the bills, we've been producing shows for other groups. We do work for the Trinity cable network. Just finished a project for the Blackwood Brothers, who perform in Branson. They'll sell videos and tapes. We've done some productions for Dale Evans and a number of other people.

"We're moving toward our own TV shows. We'll do our Sunday service. Then I plan on doing 'Gospel Country Tonight', a Johnny Carson variety type show for family channels."

The Proactive Music City Christian Fellowship

Other Christian performers in the Nashville area aren't sitting still either. The Music City Christian Fellowship was formed in 1980. Joe Babcock, leader of a quartet on Hee-Haw, and Opry star Billy Walker were elected and vice-president respectively. Stu Phillips serves as president in 1992.

Not a church, the founders stated as the purpose of the Fellowship:

To win souls to Christ through action and prayer, to encourage bold witnessing within the music and entertainment industry . . .; to provide fellowship for believers within the industry that we might be brought closer together . . .; to provide a sponsoring organization to carry out various worthwhile projects, such as evangelistic services, television programs, counseling services, a Music Row chapel and any other works and ministries that God would lead us to do; to encourage righteous living and faithful stewardship among ourselves and those around us; to influence for the good the music and entertainment industry.

At one Fellowship meeting, Marijohn Wilkin reported on a Christian novel she had just read. The book was *In His Steps Today* by Marti Hefley. Marijohn challenged her fellow believers to "try to do everything for one week the way you think Jesus would."

Bill Walker (no relation to Opry singer Billy Walker), a well-known director for Country-music specials on television, told of a recent recording session with Johnny Cash. "Johnny called me out of the group. I thought, 'Boy, what have I done now?' All he said was, 'Let's have a little prayer together.' That made my day."

Joe Babcock described a recording session in which he balked at singing an offensive word. "I messed up the record and the director flared up at me. I offered to pay for the damage, but he cooled off. However, I haven't gotten any work from him since. I'm trying to spread the word around that we don't do that kind of material."

"The percentage of Christians in [Country] music has been going up," observed Bill Walker. "We're not perfect. We're human. We're only forgiven."

In future meetings the Fellowship group discussed how to increase the Christian influence in Country music. The result was "Sunday Morning Country" to be presented by Fellowship members in the War Memorial Auditorium at the close of the annual Fan Fair.

Six hundred fans showed up. Before going on stage Billy Walker led the group in prayer. He claimed "the authority of Jesus and the Holy Spirit over every demonic force in this building."

LuLu Roman sang and gave her testimony. When emcee Bill Collie introduced Billy, a wild-looking man ran up from the audience, grabbed the microphone, and began singing a frenzied version of *How Great Thou Art*. Biff and Billy tried to get him off, but he refused to budge. Then Billy simply touched him on the forehead and prayerfully said, "Jesus!" The man became so disoriented that he had to be helped off-stage.

After he finished his song and testimony, Billy walked out-side and spotted the troubled man sitting bent over on a rail-ing. When Billy started talking to him, he went into a frenzy again and then fell to the ground several feet below. "It looked like a force threw him over," Billy says.

Billy called an ambulance to take him to the hospital and later contacted the man's wife. The couple went home to New Jersey the next weekend. Billy and his wife, Betty, put a min-ister there in touch with them and they accepted Christ.

A dozen others made professions of faith at the close of the first "Sunday Morning Country." The Fellowship decided to repeat the service at the close of the annual deejay convention in October.

This time more Christian artists, including Connie Smith and George Hamilton IV, participated with other fellowship regulars.

Billy Walker told the deejays: "We're still in the Country music business, singing our Country songs; the one thing we share in common is Jesus Christ. A few years ago I had a num-ber-one hit song. I was, of all people, most miserable. I had everything you could speak of and yet in my heart I had nothing. I said, 'What is this? Why can't I be happy? Why can't I be the kind of person I want to be?' Something spoke to me and said, *You don't have what it takes to be anything.*

"I said, 'Lord, if fame and money cannot satisfy, I want whatever will.' When I gave Christ my life, that longing was met."

Connie Smith followed with song and testimony. "My life began when I chose Jesus and became God's child. He grows sweeter and sweeter. I gave up my music. It had become a curse in ny life, but when I gave my heart to Jesus, He gave my music right back to me."

Teddy Wilburn was next. He said, "I was drunk for five-and-a-half years and maybe sober 30 evenings out of that whole time. I thought people had done me in. I couldn't cope, Instead of going to Jesus, I went to the bottle. I found no answer there. My life only continued to get worse."

"I praise God that He touched my life. I now have a personal relationship with Jesus Christ. I don't know why He loved me. But I sure do love Him."

Marijohn Wilkin was next. "I was like Teddy and Billy and Connie. I also know what it's like to find Jesus as the Savior who can heal and forgive. After I accepted Him and gave Him my life, I wondered how I could make it. He told me, 'Just follow Me one step at a time.'" She then sang *One Day at a Time* and got a standing ovation.

After more songs and testimonies Assembly of God minister Joe Dee Kelley gave a short message and invited people to accept Christ. People responded from every section of the auditorium.

After 12 years the Music City Christian Fellowship is still doing two big "Sunday Morning Country" shows a year. The 1992 Fan Fair performances attracted 3,500 people. George

Hamilton IV, Freddie Hart (who traveled from Branson), Jack Greene, and Connie Smith were among the featured performers. Stu Phillips served as emcee and gave a short gospel message.

Forecasts for the Future

Back in the 1980s Joe Babcock, a founding member of the Fellowship and a Baptist Sunday-school teacher, saw a turn for the good in Country music. A music major graduate of the University of Nebraska, Joe is talented as a writer, performer, and director of musical groups. His Nashville Additions quartet has served a a backup group for scores of top artists, on Hee-Haw and in recording studios. Joe presently directs a 40-voice "Country Corral" choir made up of Country singers, studio musicians, and "a lot of young kids who are trying to get into Country music. We do old-time Spirit-filled gospel," Joe says.

Low-key and easygoing, Joe has developed friendships with scores and scores of people in the industry both in Nashville and in Branson. He's encouraged at the positive things that are happening in Country music.

The trash keeps returning, Joe concedes. "But if just a small percentage of us Christians would tell the radio and television stations we don't like the songs they're playing and tell the recording studios that we aren't going to buy tapes and CD's that glamorize illicit sex and use language we don't like, then something will happen. I include the record companies because they want to make music that people will buy."

The way Stu Phillips saw things from the perspective of the 1980s is that "people are getting tired of the cheap sex and the way standards are flouted . . . Writing letters can help . . . The Country-music industry is very sensitive to letters. There's a lot of discussion in our [music] circles about providing good, clean family entertainment in Country shows. I really believe this Country is on the advent of some sort of reformation, but the record company executive will be the last to know."

Stu speaks as both a performer and as an ordained minister in the Nashville area.

Five-hundred miles west of Opry town is tiny Branson. Approaching from the north you can sense the modernistic First Baptist Church on a hill to the right, just beyond the junction of U.S. 65 with Missouri 76—the beginning of the Branson Strip. In his 15 years as pastor there, Jay Scribner has seen The Strip become one of the best-known thoroughfares in America. He is acquainted with many members of the Branson music community. Around 150 visitors attend his services each week.

"You don't hear any of the hard stuff on The Strip," Jay says. "The family is protected. Mega-corporations could come in and start changing all of this," he warns. "We could lose our hometown Country shows."

Though he has become a "bit concerned", Jay sees Branson continuing as an important part of the revival of family values in Country music. "People are finally getting serious about this AIDS epidemic and rampant immorality. It's slow but definite. I think we're just seeing the beginnings of a real values revival. We need it. God knows we need it."

Acknowledgements

Many persons in the Country-music industry (performers, writers, etc.) shared with me their troubles and triumphs. Not once did I ever detect that anyone was trying to evade a tough question. Their transparency was obvious; their openness was refreshing.

I received special help from the Country Music Hall of Fame's Media Center; the Nashville Public Library; the Chattanooga-Hamilton County Bicentennial Library; the University of Tennessee libraries; the public libraries in Branson and Springfield, MO; the John Edwards Foundation of Los Angeles; the Radio and Television Commission of the Southern Baptist Convention, producers of the popular radio show, *Country Crossroads*; and Dr. Richard A. Peterson, a sociologist at Vanderbilt University.

Jerry Strobel and the public relations folks at the Grand Ole Opry threw down the welcome mat. Jerry never said something couldn't be done but said, "Let's see what we can do."

Many ministers shared views on Country performers and music. These included Jimmie Snow, Billy Ray Moore, Don Finto, Ralph Stone, Joe Dee Kelley, Jay Scribner, and Joe Johnson, the funniest editor at the Baptist Sunday School Board.

Special appreciation goes to writer-colleague Ginny Waddell, who has done scores of articles on Country-music personalities in Nashville. Hollye Stosberg, director of public relations for the Baldknobbers Hillbilly Jamboree Show, was helpful in Branson.

A big thank-you to all of the above, plus many others who helped make possible the writing of this book.